CORPORA
COMMUNI
INVOLVEME...

philanthropy or self-interest?

DELWIN ROY

CW00471889

© 1999 Charities Aid Foundation

Published by Charities Aid Foundation
Kings Hill
West Malling
Kent ME19 4TA

Tel +44 1732 520000
Fax +44 1732 520001
Website http://www.charitynet.org
E-mail cafpubs@caf.charitynet.org

Editor Caroline Hartnell

Design and production GreenGate Publishing Services, Tonbridge, Kent

Cover design Eugenie Dodd Typographics

Printed and bound by Bell & Bain, Glasgow

A catalogue record for this book is available from the British Library.

ISBN 1–85934–101–2

Contents

About the author   4

Acknowledgements   5

1 Introduction   7

2 CCI in the global competitive landscape of the twenty-first century   15

3 Serving business self-interest through CCI: the debate   24

4 CCI worldwide: emerging themes and practices   31

5 Good corporate citizenship: the broader picture   54

6 The future of corporate citizenship, the future of capitalism 67

Notes   71

About CAF   72

Other publications from CAF   76

Index   78

About the author

D r Delwin A Roy is the Founding President and CEO Emeritus of The Hitachi Foundation. Formed in 1985 by Hitachi Ltd, the Foundation is a programmatically diverse, private corporate foundation, and the largest of the Japanese-funded foundations established in the United States.

Prior to this Dr Roy undertook a wide variety of international assignments – for USAID (in Uruguay and Argentina) and the Ford Foundation (Egypt, Lebanon, Jordan, Saudi Arabia, Kuwait, Yemen Arab Republic, and Sudan) among others. From 1978 to 1981 he was the first director of the International Business Council, a university-system-based business and economic research organization. In 1981, as Chief Executive Officer, he founded Development Decisions International, an economic development and international business development group serving clients such as USAID, the World Bank and Harvard Institute for International Development.

Dr Roy has authored works on management, economic development policy, political economy, privatization, and global corporate responsibility. He co-authored *Global Corporate Citizenship: Rationale and strategies* (Hitachi Foundation, 1997).

Acknowledgements

The material for this work was gained in large part from my experience in building Hitachi Corporation's citizenship agenda in the United States and globally. I owe Elliot L Richardson, chairman of the Hitachi Foundation, and Dr Katsushige Mita, Chairman Emeritus, Hitachi Ltd, a vote of thanks. I was given considerable latitude in developing this agenda and enjoyed their personal support throughout its implementation.

The effort of the many capable staff members drawn to the vision which has guided the work of the Foundation must also be recognized. The dedication and professionalism they have brought to this work is extraordinary.

I wish to give a special thanks to Laurie Regelbrugge, vice-president of the Hitachi Foundation. Her comments and suggestions on early drafts of this work were of inestimable value.

1 Introduction

'Seventy corporations now rank bigger than many a nation-state – will they grow bigger still? Does that matter?'
Charles Handy, 'A Better Capitalism', *Across the Board* (April 1998).

'We came to the point of view that our real rationale should be to focus on issues that had a direct relevance to the long-term success of our business.'
Mary Stewart Hall, former VP, Corporate Contributions, Weyerhauser Co.

'I think that it is immoral to give away the shareholders' money; such charitable actions are for the private individual to undertake.'
Ronnie Chan, Chairman, Hang Lung Development Group (Hong Kong), *Conference on Corporate Citizenship in the Asia-Pacific.*

'I know of no better economic system [capitalism]. Nevertheless, the new fashion of turning everything into a business, even our own lives, doesn't seem to be the answer.'
Charles Handy, ' A Better Capitalism', *Across the Board* (April 1998).

'It may be tainted money, but t'ain't enough!'
Mark Twain.

After almost 13 years at the helm of a new corporate foundation, the Hitachi Foundation, I have one major observation to make about corporate philanthropy. Unless one is able to demonstrate clearly to the management of a business that establishes a corporate community involvement (CCI) programme **how** this programme is of benefit to the company, and the many stakeholders in this company, it is unlikely that whatever investments are being made in the community will be taken seriously. This benefit can come from community contributions that are purely altruistic in intent, seeking no business advantage whatsoever. It can also come from community contributions that are patently linked to business strategies. And, of course, it can come from contributions that serve a high moral purpose and public need and also serve business interests.

If a business is at its best when it is 'strategic' in thinking through the growth scenarios that lead to expanding markets and sales growth, increases in productivity, lower production costs and higher product quality, why is it assumed that being 'strategic' about its community involvement – and deriving business benefit from this – is somehow unacceptable?

Having a strategy simply means that specific objectives, based on study and analysis of the alternatives, are pursued through a decisive set of actions. In CCI, 'being strategic' can simply mean seeking every opportunity to link a corporation's name to its community investments. Or it may mean linking a cause to a specific product, or choosing to support education reform because it believes that the labour supply upon which it depends must be first rate. Many think that being strategic is inconsistent with the 'giving spirit'. As Jack Shakely, of California Community Foundation, notes: 'Philanthropy is supposed to be just that, with nothing coming back, other than immortality, for the donor.'

I believe that a firm seriously thinking through its contributions to the community – even choosing to consider these as 'investments' rather than donations or gifts – is being strategic in its investment approach and is more likely to bring added value both to the community and to itself. An investment that receives good planning, seeks to measure impact on community problems, and commands the attention of top management and full organizational support for the initiative is far preferable to the alternative. The philanthropic landscape around the world is littered with the remains of thousands of projects, some achieving extraordinary results, because these projects could not be sustained or maintain the needed benefactor interest for long-term constructive results.

I acknowledge that engaging businesses on the basis of a company's self-interest involves risk to communities. The negotiation of mutually beneficial projects may suffer from an imbalance of power and resources, with the result that the community is not always able to deal from strength. The smart company will not take advantage in such situations, but malice and predation do on rare occasion surface. At times, such circumstances stem more from an overly exuberant marketing or public relations department than from any attempt to manipulate representatives of community organizations. Nevertheless, in such situations great damage can be done.

But one should not assume that this negotiating imbalance always favours the business seeking strategic business results from a community investment. If the need for the project or programme is significant to the business, it may be the community that is best able to negotiate for its needs.

This examination of CCI presents a wealth of case material, used to examine the motivations at work when companies support community-based actions – though it is necessarily selective, for thousands of actions by hundreds of corporations take place worldwide every year.

Discussion of CCI is placed in the context of changes taking place globally. Much of the rationale set forth for placing strategic business value on a company's CCI activity stems from the rapid changes that have taken place in the global economy. Not every international corporation chooses to practise CCI beyond the shores of its home country. However, there is increasing evidence that many of these corporations feel that practising

CCI may be one way of competing for new foreign markets. Whether companies choose to confine their CCI programmes to the domestic marketplace or expand these to new foreign markets, the effects of global competition are influencing corporate attitudes. This does not mean that all companies will adopt a CCI strategy. It does mean that they have to carefully review alternative ways of being corporately responsible in the twenty-first century.

Why do companies engage in CCI?

There are many ways that CCI is practised and a number of terms used to refer to it: corporate citizenship, community action, community affairs, community investment, community relations, corporate affairs, corporate philanthropy, corporate grant-making, public affairs, external affairs, and direct contributions. Irrespective of terminology, CCI comprises focused corporate activities designed to create an external benefit or a mutual benefit to the business and an external entity.

The practice of giving, or giving back, varies considerably from one cultural setting to the next. The political regime, the rule of law and particular religious beliefs all flavour the practice. Most cultures have some form of charitable giving in evidence. And, in almost all instances, business participates in this tradition – whether in the form of individual giving from wealth accumulated through business or in the form of the company taking action as a company. The practice of corporate philanthropy as well as the broader practice of corporate citizenship is in part conditioned by the cultural setting in which it occurs, in its home country or abroad.

Chris Marsden, in his foreword to *Global Corporate Citizenship: Rationale and strategies*,[1] eloquently sets out the primary reasons why companies, in his words, '*must* participate' in supporting communities:

- To improve corporate reputation with local communities, opinion leaders and customers.
- To derive benefits that accrue to employees through opportunities to volunteer and render public service.
- To establish business and community contacts, build alliances with stakeholders – shareholders, suppliers, employees, public leaders and customers – and gain important business management knowledge by better understanding the local operating environment.
- To take advantage of direct marketing opportunities where CCI activities can logically and openly be tied to business interests.

To this list I would add three other reasons why businesses engage in CCI activities. These derive in large part from the changes that have taken place competitively and politically and are perhaps most germane to those undertaking business operations in the newly emerging markets:

- To build a sustainable market presence over time by investing in the social infrastructure to ensure healthy and productive human resource capability and healthy community environments for long-term free-market development.
- To build upon the capacity of NGOs and governments to provide important infrastructure needs such as adequate housing, medical care, education and training and such services as potable water, sanitation and transportation.
- To build effective partnerships between the government, NGOs and the private corporate sector to achieve what Marsden calls 'a critical mass – an effective three-way partnership – each bringing their resources, expertise and perspective to the problem'.

The degree to which any one of these motives prevails in building the internal support and rationale for an active citizenship agenda varies considerably. Some activities – cause-related marketing, for example – relate directly to a business agenda and market strategy. Others, such as providing volunteering opportunities to employees, are less direct in their effect on business interests but can nevertheless contribute greatly to employee morale and, in some cases, to retaining qualified personnel.

Variety in the rationale given and CCI strategies pursued is clearly apparent, not just across industries but within industry categories. Since innovation is perhaps one of the greatest strengths the private sector can bring to its CCI programmes, a high degree of diversity in the social causes and issues supported and the manner of support should probably be viewed as a strength.

When is the combination of motivations likely to be best, not only for the business but for the organizations – and the social causes and concerns on their agendas – that a company chooses to support? Chris Marsden answers this by noting: 'To build a critical mass of the business sector to make significant and sustainable contributions, it is best to work with the grain of normal business motivation rather than rely solely on a sense of civic duty or philanthropy.' I know of very few engaged in the practice of corporate citizenship who would disagree with this.

The degree to which a business seeks specific self-interest and bottom-line impact through its CCI activities is conditioned by the cultural context from which the business comes and its particular business culture. Businesses in the USA, foreign or domestic, have considerably more flexibility and motivation to support education than businesses in France, where the government is indisposed to allow even French corporations to engage actively in this field. While in Japan corporations are proscribed from making a broad range of investments in social causes and community needs – health care, housing, education, crime prevention or substance abuse prevention – Japanese corporations are expected to do so through their operations in the USA, but not in France.

Businesses vary widely, wherever they conduct operations, in the degree to which they want or are permitted to link their CCI programmes to their business interests. In the USA, the legal framework makes such links possible and relatively easy; in other parts of the world, establishing such links may be far more problematic. In China, for example, donations and other forms of charitable giving to government officials or other persons with influence over government actions for the express purpose of gaining business favour are treated in the foreign investment law as acts of bribery, and in the extreme are punishable by death.[2] Some nations have legal prohibitions enacted to prevent businesses from engaging in bribery for the purpose of gaining competitive advantage. In the USA, the Foreign Corrupt Practices Act is one such law. It certainly applies to any payment that is in fact an attempt to bribe that a business tries to pass off as a charitable action or community contribution.

What methods do companies use to promote CCI goals and objectives?

There are a number of methods that companies use in their CCI programmes. In some countries, such as the USA and the UK, wide latitude and discretion are given to the business sector in selecting methods. In other countries, such as those of continental Europe, there tend to be fewer avenues by which a corporation is permitted to engage in corporate giving. In some cases, there are limits to the kinds of causes to which a business may give; in others, there are limits as to what a company can give (cash, equipment, volunteer time, etc). Finally, tax incentives – where these exist – often provide additional motivation to contribute to specific issues and causes to which the state attaches importance.

CASH TRANSFERS

These include:

- grants, either for the operating expenses of non-profit organizations (NPOs) or for a particular programme or action;
- employee matching funds programmes, which allow individual employees to select a cause to which they wish to contribute and the company 'matches' their contribution (usually according to a formula such as 1:1, 2:3);

- donations and contributions, which are different from grants in that few if any conditions attach to the 'gift';
- payroll giving systems, which allow employees to make regular payments to NPOs directly from their pay (the company may also match such contributions);
- sponsorships for sports, arts and other cultural events.

NON-CASH AND 'NEAR' CASH EQUIVALENCIES

These include:

- company-sponsored employee volunteer services, which may be on a release-time basis;
- provision of supplies to volunteers performing community service;
- provision of expertise to NPOs in organization and management, finance, marketing, public relations and communications, small-scale (micro-credit) business start-up, and production through an executive-in-residence or on a non-residence basis;
- provision of specialized technical assistance in fields such as engineering and medicine;
- mentoring services (particularly in school-to-work programmes);
- service on NPO boards of directors;
- free use of office space and equipment, telecommunications;
- provision of office supplies, instructional materials and meeting facilities;
- in-kind donations of products of all kinds, including new and used office equipment;
- making transportation services available;
- providing access to printing and publication services;
- transfer of company shares (stock equities) to NPO portfolios.

CAPITAL AND INTERMEDIATE CAPITAL GOODS TRANSFERS

These include:

- capital goods such as buildings and other physical plant (equipped laboratories, sports facilities, etc) provided to educational institutions (commonly called 'bricks and mortar' contributions);
- funds for revolving loans to finance microcredit start-ups;
- intermediate capital goods such as excess micro-chip inventories contributed to laboratories on campus for use in engineering and science education.

Businesses can use any combination of these methods in providing community support. Worldwide, the causes that receive the most corporate funding include education, culture and the arts, and medical and health research and care. Within education, the two most frequently used methods of giving support are the provision of scholarships and student and teacher exchange programmes.

VOLUNTEERING

Today one observes a growing worldwide trend for businesses to emphasize a 'more than cash giving' approach. Employee volunteerism is widely favoured, as most companies recognize that one of their chief assets is their employee base. It is increasingly believed that a policy of encouraging volunteer activity (and one, in particular, that allows for paid release-time and provides supplies to volunteers) is key to retaining qualified personnel and maintaining a high level of employee morale.

Employee volunteering is not necessarily favoured in all parts of the world. One finds transnational corporations prone to adapt where volunteer activity is a tradition and to eschew it where it is not. Japanese corporations operating in the USA are a good example. Almost every Japanese corporation with a community presence in the USA emphasizes volunteerism. The Japan External Trade Organization (JETRO) conducts an annual survey of all US-based Japanese corporations and delineates all forms of volunteer activity conducted by their employees. But the primary focus on volunteerism has been largely in the USA because of the well-established tradition of volunteerism. Elsewhere in the world, Japanese corporations are far less active, and, if they are active, volunteerism tends not to be a primary means by which they engage in CCI.

What is a 'responsible' corporation?

There are any number of corporations that are recognized as being 'responsible corporate citizens': US firms such as Merck & Co (pharmaceuticals), Levi Strauss & Company (apparel) and Hewlett-Packard (computer technology); UK and continental European firms such as Marks & Spencer (retail department stores), the Swiss company Ciba-Geigy (chemicals and pharmaceuticals), the German company Robert Bosch GmbH (communications technology, automotive equipment), and the French company ELF-Aquitaine (petroleum products); Japanese firms such as Hitachi Ltd (power distribution equipment, computers, bullet trains) and Honda Motor Corporation (automobiles); and firms in emerging markets such as the Philippine company Ayala Corporation (insurance, finance, housing construction), the Brazilian company Aracruz Cellulose SA (paper pulp), the Jamaican company ICWI Group (insurance, finance and real estate) and the Turkish company the Koc Group (transportation products, banking and finance, retailing).

What makes these firms, and hundreds of others, stand out and leads to their recognition as 'good corporate citizens'? There is no single factor, but in the area of CCI it is usually the long-term, organization-wide commitment to be a good corporate citizen, both in terms of the quality of products provided and in the civic sense. In some cases, this commitment stems from the vision of the founder(s). In others, management has realized the business value of striving to be a good and involved corporate citizen.

When are companies considered 'irresponsible'? There are many examples: when Royal Dutch Shell fails to be sensitive to environmental concerns, whether in the North Sea (sinking an obsolescent drilling platform) or in Nigeria (polluting the environment and dealing with odious and repressive military regimes); Exxon on the occasion of the *Exxon Valdez* oil spill; Union Carbide in the Bhopal incident; General Electric for ostensibly dumping old lead batteries in the Philippines; and any number of Japanese firms for damaging the environment throughout South-East Asia by using 'slash and burn' tactics in stripping resources such as hardwood forests.

It is important to note that in many cases where corporate irresponsibility is charged, the companies had excellent reputations as good corporate citizens *prior* to the incidents that led to public criticism. One must also note that status as a good citizen has once again been accorded many firms *since* the incidents that led to public disapproval occurred.

In most countries, the practice of corporate citizenship remains a very minor sideshow. The state is expected to resolve the major community needs for development, growth and prosperity. However, the enormous growth of the private sector is changing this scenario. Even though the impact of this growth falls very unevenly around the world, there is an impact.

In my opinion, in the long term, the private sector must take real responsibility for the creation of healthy communities and a healthy environment. Either the 'market' that so many firms slavishly follow in determining their business practices will enforce this or public reaction and pressure exerted on governments will. Most likely, it will be a combination of both.

In my opinion, most companies take their responsibilities seriously. As a colleague of mine, Roger Regelbrugge, CEO, GS Industries, a Kuwaiti-owned US-based international holding company (steel products, mining, retailing), notes: 'I don't know of too many CEOs who sit around trying to figure out how to make their corporations *irresponsible* [emphasis mine].' I think that he is right.

2 CCI in the global competitive landscape of the twenty-first century

These days, the issue of whether corporations and businesses should seek strategic business interest or competitive advantage through their CCI efforts is often debated in the non-profit sector. Characteristically labelled the 'bottom line', it is argued that while businesses must indeed make a profit, the 'profit motive' should not attach to whatever actions may be taking place with respect to investment, or reinvestment, in the community. Many take the view that this deviation from the altruistic to the profitable is dangerous and unwarranted.

Yet another line of thinking on the relationship between the need and the ability to compete, particularly on a global scale, and the corresponding need for a company's community and social investments to be strategically positioned to serve this need and ability, has emerged in the past ten years and is gaining momentum.

It is useful to give this sense of departure from the 'altruistic' to the 'profitable' a historical perspective. An example drawn from the US experience illustrates this evolution.

From altruism to corporate strategy

The US government has never really sought to control large segments of the private economy nor has it ever had a strong socialist constituency in the political process. Taxation of the private sector has been kept intentionally low, considerably lower than in either Western Europe or Asia where national governments are expected to provide extensive social welfare programmes. It is not surprising, then, that one finds that corporate philanthropy in Europe and Asia is on a considerably smaller scale than in the US.

This propensity to keep corporate taxation low is in part tied to the expectation that the private corporate sector *will* make philanthropic or social investments in America's communities. Tax breaks on corporate charitable contributions have been provided to ensure that these transfer payments are made. The US government does not specify to what causes or purposes these transfers should be directed, requiring only that those receiving them be 'qualified as legitimate and legally established not-for-profit organizations'.

Up to 1985 or so, it generally did not seem to matter what causes a business was supporting nor what impact its giving was having. Evidence that a company was giving for charitable purposes seemed adequate. The organizations receiving financial support were quite happy that companies generally attached few or no conditions to the funds being dispensed.

I am not suggesting that in this formative stage of the development of corporate giving business interests were not being served through corporate charitable actions. For example, revisions in the 1982 tax law allowed US corporations giving in-kind donations, ie products, to accelerate the write-off of such product donations and allowed them to use a product cost calculation that was more proximate to the market price than actual cost in order to capture larger tax benefits. The only requirement was that the in-kind gifts be made to education institutions, particularly higher education. Firms such as Apple Computer, Hewlett-Packard and IBM benefited greatly from what in effect was a subsidized product marketing promotion: these firms were able to educate future consumers on their products.

Cause-related marketing, the practice of tying product sales to support for a specific cause, first began in the 1980s. The American Express Company is credited with this innovation, linking use of its credit card first to the restoration of Ellis Island in New York City and subsequently to the Arc de Triomphe in Paris. Sponsorships of sports and arts events increased, with companies often requiring the company name and products to be featured through displays and other advertising gambits.

What has changed?

The economic ascendancy of Japan in the 1980s served notice on the USA that its position of world economic dominance was being challenged. Market share was no longer simply a matter of the company's position in its respective national economy; competition had become global. The drive for low-cost production and developments in technology were rapidly leading to an almost unmitigated free flow of capital worldwide.

Three major factors have begun to alter the role of the private sector, not just in the USA but in Europe and in the emerging economies, particularly those in the Asia Pacific region.

- Competitive change on a global scale has irrevocably altered the way in which corporations must compete. Global supply chains have increased the number of businesses involved geometrically. By 1997 there were more than 40,000 transnational companies identified as opposed to about 7,000 in 1975. These transnational companies are linked to over 200,000 affiliates and subsidiaries located throughout the world.
- New technologies, particularly information technologies, have enabled

corporations to move administrative, sales and service, and production facilities at will.

■ National governments are less able to meet the demand for high-quality and effective services of their citizenry.

Cumulatively, these forces have influenced the practice of CCI. Given the extraordinary changes since the early 1980s, the question ought not to be 'Why are companies changing their giving practices and seeking greater complementarity between their business aims and their CCI actions?' but rather 'Why wouldn't they?'

What changes when a company elects to be more 'strategic' in its CCI?

I use the expression 'more' strategic because I conclude that any company practising CCI is already being 'strategic' in one sense or another. If, for example, a firm chooses not to engage in CCI in a particular location, or not to support a particular community issue or cause, it is still 'being strategic'. It has decided that it doesn't need to engage in CCI in that area or doesn't wish to be identified with a particular issue or cause. The term 'more' applies to yet another decision: a firm may for a variety of reasons feel compelled to justify to its various constituencies either its lack of involvement or a decision to increase its CCI budget. For example, after an oil spill, Exxon becomes the most environmentally sensitive of oil companies. It thus becomes 'more' strategic, taking great care in identifying environmental causes it now needs to support but didn't wish to support prior to the spill.

It has already been stated that there is an element of business self-interest in every corporate action that is taken in the name of community investment, responsibility or citizenship. In this chapter, I further suggest that, given the dramatic changes taking place in competition, companies must now consider whether in *any* such action, this self-interest should be more pronounced, the project or programme *more* directly aligned with specific business goals and purposes, the impact of social and community investments *measured and evaluated* in terms of quantifiable business impact as well as community improvement.

Does this in fact constitute a *new* emphasis? Or is it simply that companies now choose to be more open in emphasizing what has always been the case? The public good should be served if possible, but so too should the main goal of the company: to be profitable.

The new strategic philanthropy at work

In the United States, the business motivation has never really been absent from the practice of CCI. Even during the halcyon days of the Watson family at IBM there was nevertheless an intrinsic business logic at work that placed thousands of pieces of IBM equipment in schools and universities.

It is equally apparent that what we are talking about is a matter of the *degree of emphasis* placed on the business purpose vis-à-vis the social purpose in corporate giving. There has not been a wholesale departure from serving the social good in the US. From company to company one sees vastly different degrees of emphasis on the business motivations at work. Levi Strauss & Company emphasizes the social purpose side of the equation more than does the Coca Cola Company. Ciba-Geigy has had its giving traditions solidly rooted in social purposes since its founding, but after 1990 the company shifted to be 'more competitive in the global market place' and correspondingly changed some of its giving priorities, primarily to ensure that licence to operate was more easily acquired 'in particularly sensitive markets' (eg in Third World countries). The Hitachi Group of Companies, which operates six foundations in Japan to which *no business purpose* will ever attach, created a foundation in the USA – one of its most important markets – in part to make Japanese investment in American communities more acceptable, a clear business purpose.

For the most part, all these companies are simply responding to major changes in the way they need to compete, globally and locally.

At the same time, against the background of a general trend of moving away from sole reliance on governments to provide quality public services – as envisaged by Reagan and Thatcher, and more recently even by the French government – the private sector is now expected to carry more of the community investment and social services burden. The move towards greater emphasis on business goals in CCI activities does not conflict with these pressures. In fact I submit that business is most likely to find solutions to social issues when it is able to consider the issues within the context it knows best – business.

It is instructive to end this discussion on the 'bottom line' and CCI by looking at two cases of CCI action that demonstrate the interplay between global competitive change and what has been called 'The New Corporate Philanthropy'. Craig Smith has noted that 'more and more companies are supporting movements for social change while advancing their business goals'.[3] These cases are drawn from US corporate experience, but both are fairly representative of what other companies, US and foreign, are doing.

WAL-MART STORES INC

Wal-Mart Stores Inc operates discount department stores and 'Supercentres', a combination of full-line supermarket and discount department store centres. Over 2,000 Wal-Mart outlets are operated in the USA and in six foreign countries. Its sales exceed $33 billion and it employs 825,000 people.

The media has prominently featured resistance to several proposed openings of Wal-Mart outlets. Most often this resistance occurs in US communities, but there have also been cases in other countries, particularly in China and Mexico.

This negative public reaction is rooted primarily in the fear that the presence of a Wal-Mart store or supercentre will drive small local retailers out of business. It is sometimes even suggested that a Wal-Mart facility degrades the environment. On occasion, the resistance prevents construction of a new facility; however, usually it does not. In proposed foreign locations, public resistance is also somewhat xenophobic, and as a result couched in terms of not wanting such a crass display of consumerism as is represented by Wal-Mart – especially in countries where per capita income is low and poverty widespread.

Wal-Mart clearly has a major public relations problem with which it must deal. Recently CNN Headline News (23 April 1998 edition), which is broadcast worldwide, carried a leader at the bottom of the TV screen, citing the following as one of its 'newsworthy' events:

'Wal-Mart gives West Dover Elementary School [Delaware] *$300 grant to go whale watching.'*

This leader ran continuously through each half-hour news segment so this particular story appeared seven to nine times over a period of 24 hours throughout the world.

Is this a business self-interest message? Without a doubt: it projects Wal-Mart as a caring, youth education-oriented, environmentally concerned corporate citizen. Given that a $300 grant is not truly newsworthy, one must conclude that Wal-Mart public relations staff arranged this – or, to the extent that luck was involved, that they were more than ready to exploit its usefulness to the company.

How useful is such massive media coverage? Is there a bottom-line return? While this kind of news coverage most probably would not put a stop to public criticism of Wal-Mart, it certainly won't hurt on this score either. One might even be inclined to call this entire scenario an innovative stroke of PR genius. Wal-Mart is portrayed as 'warm and cuddly', truly concerned about our environment, our children and our schools. It suggests that a multi-billion-dollar corporation that conducts business on a global scale can nevertheless take time to reach down to a small school in a small town and make a difference: it has a 'heart'. All for only $300!

WHIRLPOOL CORPORATION

The Whirlpool Corporation manufactures home appliances and related products marketed in the USA and in every major geographical region worldwide. In 1998 its sales were more than $5 billion; it employs 61,400 people.

By the late 1980s, Whirlpool had become a leading manufacturer and marketer of major home appliances. These are produced in 13 countries and marketed under 11 different brand names in more than 140 countries. The corporation does not have a direct CCI programme; all its corporate giving is conducted through the Whirlpool Foundation, established in 1951.

Prior to 1991, its giving was solely in the USA at plants located in 11 communities in five states. Although the corporation did have international operations, the programme focus could not be said to be international. The employee matching gifts programme was confined to US employees and, as noted, no grant funds were being allocated to production or marketing units operating abroad.

After 1991, the corporation sought to make its corporate giving both more strategic and more global. While it had operations in Europe, its visibility was limited. It had considerable interest in expanding into the burgeoning markets of Asia, particularly China. It therefore confronted the question of how to reorganize its CCI programme, through its foundation, to accord with its growth ambitions internationally, in both established and new markets.

The corporation had no international grant-making experience. It concluded that the best way to gain knowledge about what would be an appropriate international giving stance was to incorporate its strategic marketing development information needs in established and emerging markets in whatever initial CCI actions it might take. The key components of the ensuing effort are interesting and informative.

Choosing the focus – women's attitudes

The company decided that the Foundation would focus on women and women's attitudes towards work, the family and society. Why?

- Most of its employees are women, women influence the design, use and sale of the company's products, and women are the core of lifestyle changes in family life.
- Gaining information about women worldwide would provide important data for future domestic and international grant-making; it would also provide input for product design, marketing and advertising, research and development, and strategic planning.

Choosing the means – research

The key instrument for generating this important social and business information would be research. Why?

- The company knew very little about women's attitudes in either its domestic or its foreign markets.
- Generating survey data would also yield extensive data that could be made available to the public. Publishing this data would be viewed as a public service.

Defining scope and process – three regions

It initially chose to conduct its research in North America, to be followed by a similar approach in Europe and Asia. Why?

- The North American and European markets were well established, those in Asia, less so. In China the market was hardly established at all.
- Focusing on the USA, Canada and Mexico in a pilot phase would allow the company researcher to test survey instruments and adjust them as necessary for external market areas.
- Europe would follow, thereby creating a rather long time frame over which the company would benefit by the serial release of region-specific research data, rather than making one big simultaneous effort in all three regions. In effect, and in business terms, this would lead to a longer shelf life for the research product cumulatively.

Repositioning the foundation – a new global strategic approach to CCI

A successful result, one that yielded a better understanding of women, would also position the Whirlpool Foundation as a strategic market information resource to the corporation. How?

- All the major corporate departments and levels would become party to a strategic approach to CCI.
- Customer services, advertising and marketing, and production planning would benefit from a better understanding of customers.
- Human resource development would benefit from a better understanding of the largest component of the workforce – women. This would bring new thinking to training and development, and recognition of the need to incorporate diversity in the workforce and gender parity in access to promotions and top-management positions.
- Public and government relations departments would have considerable information with which to influence public policy, to demonstrate corporate concern with affirmative action agendas, and, if so inclined, human, women's and civil rights.

Project outcomes

- The research was conducted; 3,000 men and women in North America, and 7,000 men and women in five European countries, were interviewed.

- Thousands of copies of the reports were disseminated in five different languages.

- Extensive press coverage raised the identity of the Foundation and the visibility of its commitment to women's issues. This enabled it to build new partnerships in key areas and to begin, in 1996, to make informed and targeted grants in these market areas – even in the North American market where the Foundation had long been established.

- On the corporate side, management is using the findings to design new advertising messages, to improve communication (internal and external), and to improve policies to recruit, retain and promote women workers. Employees report increased pride and morale, and a correspondingly higher commitment to their employer.

This is 'bottom line' oriented CCI, but it is also something else. This approach performed an important public information role. It made a corporate giving effort more relevant to the company as a whole and it made all major departments stakeholders in a strategic data-generating project on critical social issues of importance worldwide. The corporation as a result is better informed and the Foundation is making better use of its scarce and limited resources, again worldwide. It resulted in the corporation taking its CCI more seriously internally; the global citizenship effort is no longer viewed as 'chequebook philanthropy' or 'the give-away game'.

The Whirlpool Foundation was thus transformed in a matter of four years from a somewhat benign operation with an endowment of $10 million and an annual contributions budget of $3 million to one with an endowment of $20 million and a grants budget of $7.5 million. This seems to have happened because people in the company recognized the importance of the CCI function: improvements in employee morale and the increased global visibility of the firm were clearly tangible benefits. The corporation's goal had been to move away from being just an ordinary supporter of 'safe' projects, and that goal was attained: Whirlpool went from giving Little League teams a $500 donation to supporting the conduct of important social research in its major world market areas. It thus made 'strategic' sense to make more assets available to the CCI function.

The results of the Foundation's third effort, a survey on the attitudes of children to their mothers' multiple roles in contemporary society, was published on 16 April 1998. On 6 May 1998 the *Ladies' Home Journal*, a leading family magazine in the USA, announced a contest supported by a $500,000 grant from Whirlpool to identify mothers who succeed in juggling multiple roles as income providers and care-givers. In addition, Whirlpool recently announced a $1 million Fund for Families. Those seeking funds to further research on children's attitudes to their mothers can submit proposals to the Foundation.

As a result of this extraordinary effort of the company and the Foundation, the head of the Foundation has been promoted to a line-management position as Director of Brand Development for Whirlpool's KitchenAid line of products. Not bad.

3 Serving business self-interest through CCI: the debate

The issues and observations addressed thus far are not found only in the US corporate experience. Globalization does lead to a degree of convergence in the way in which companies conduct international business. Technological advances alone would account for this convergence – although companies must also adapt to the particular culture in which they do business.

This convergence does not necessarily attach to CCI practices. However, the debate regarding the uses and possible abuses of a strategic, business-related approach to citizenship action is proving far more universal than any accepted norms for company behaviour – at least, thus far.

I recall a conference in September 1995, on Corporate Citizenship in the Asia Pacific, which illustrates the global character of the business self-interest debate. More than 100 representatives of Asian, US, European, Australian and Canadian corporations attended. Excerpts from the presentations on the opening day demonstrate the wide range of perspectives on the mandate for and character of corporate citizenship in their vast region.

- **Sung-Joo Han**, former Minister of Foreign Affairs, Republic of Korea: 'Governments should carry the main burden of coping with change. Yet, as the relative weight of the role and importance of the private sector vis-à-vis the government sector increases, corporations have both the responsibility and opportunity to step in.'
- **Ronnie Chan**, Chairman, Hang Lung Development Group (Hong Kong): 'Cultural, religious and family traditions in Asia have long been the reasons for individual charitable giving. The sole purpose of the corporation is to make a profit, increase market growth and, therefore, returns to shareholders. Only if corporate giving contributes to these goals, does such giving make sense. I think that it is immoral and illegal to give away shareholders' money.'
- **Jaime Augusto Zobel de Ayala II**, President, Ayala Corporation and Ayala Foundation (Philippines): 'To Mr Chan I can only say that we do not have the luxury in the Philippines of making such fine distinctions between high morals, profitable purpose and the obligation of businesses to help with the issues of poverty, education and housing. Of course, business should be concerned with bringing solutions to difficult problems based on its business expertise, but producing positive

outcomes does not have to be closely allied with strategic business goals and objectives.'

▪ **Mr Yotaro Kobayashi**, Chairman and CEO, Fuji Xerox Co (Japan): 'In Fuji Xerox we have an active programme promoting volunteerism among our employees in Japan; this is not usual for a Japanese company. Corporations do have a major role to play to create healthy communities, but "enlightened self-interest" must go well beyond market performance as the only responsibility of business. Where great social needs exist, particularly in emerging economies, this self-interest must be much more than just a business and profit concern.'[4]

Until the recent (1998) major economic downturn in Asian countries, corporate giving was the most rapidly growing component of philanthropy in the region, although it is of considerably less magnitude than is to be found in the USA or Europe. Many, within and outside the Asia Pacific region, do not expect the economic troubles to reverse this trend; some expect it to accelerate. But the motivations for giving do appear to be very different from in the Western industrialized countries. If 'business interest' influences corporate citizenship in the Asia Pacific, it is only in ways secondary to more important communal, social and humanitarian motivations.

Survey data on corporate attitudes towards the rationale for CCI underline the East-West differences. Table 1 contrasts motivations between the USA, Japan and Europe.

Table 1 Why do corporations do it? (%)

	Total	US	Japan	Europe
There must be a combination of community benefits and benefits for the corporation	63	67	53	68
CCI is a subtle form of promotional activity that benefits my corporation directly	55	58	40	68
It is enough that it benefits the community	28	30	39	16
It must directly contribute to selling more products/services	19	18	17	23

Source Bozell Worldwide, Wall Street Journal International, Nihon Keizai Shimbun. As cited in D Logan, D Roy and L Regelbrugge (1997) *Global Corporate Citizenship: Rationale and strategies*, Hitachi Foundation.

Based on this survey of transnational corporations, firms in Western Europe seem more comfortable with the 'business self-interest' motivation, ranking the highest on the use of community support activities for promotional and sales outcomes.

Table 2 presents the results of a more recent survey, reported by Chris Marsden in *Alliance* (March 1997).[5] Business managers were asked whether business goals were the primary *raison d'être* of corporations in their home countries or 'whether, besides making a profit, a company had a goal of attaining the well-being of its various stakeholders'.

Table 2 Profit motive vis-à-vis stakeholder well-being*
(% responding profit only)

USA	Australia	Canada	UK		
40	35	34	33		
Italy	*Sweden*	*Netherlands*	*Belgium*	*Germany*	*France*
28	27	26	25	24	16
Singapore	*Japan*				
11	8				

* The data are configured somewhat differently from the way they were presented by Marsden.

Marsden observes that managers coming from an Anglo-Saxon environment are a bit more business-minded than those coming from continental Europe and 'utterly different' from those in Japan and Singapore. This survey data appears to be reasonably consistent with that presented in Table 1 and the comments of those cited from the conference on Corporate Citizenship in the Asia Pacific. Culture, religious values and communitarian beliefs obviously matter, and differences in these have a significant effect on the degree to which business self-interest is acceptable as a rationale for CCI activity.

Is the US model driving convergence in transnational CCI behaviour?

Corporate giving in the USA remains somewhat of an anomaly when compared to that in other countries. It might reasonably be argued that since corporate giving is both encouraged and stimulated by US government policy and public expectation, it is therefore more free to pursue business interests through its citizenship practices.

This may well be the case, but US firms operating abroad have to be careful to adapt to local culture and public attitudes. For example, cause-related marketing may be accepted in the USA, but less so in Europe and not at all in Asia. Conversely, foreign investors coming to the USA will quickly learn that business-related motives can acceptably play a larger part in their CCI activities.

US-BASED JAPANESE FIRMS: AN EXAMPLE OF COUNTER-CULTURE CCI BEHAVIOUR

Japanese corporations operating in the USA are a good example of the latter. Beginning in the early 1980s, a number of major Japanese corporations started to form corporate foundations and direct contributions programmes. Such practices were not unknown in Japan, but there were few incentives for Japanese corporations to establish them. The Japanese government has little appetite for the formation of an active independent sector, at least to the extent that growth of such a sector would be interpreted as a failure of the national government to provide adequately the services the Japanese public needs and expects. Corporate foundations do exist in Japan, but they are severely limited in what they can do. Certainly, pursuing business interest through corporate giving is not acceptable in Japan, as the results of a 1992 survey show.

Table 3 Reasons for involvement in philanthropy in Japan by Japanese corporations

% giving a positive response

Responsibility as a member of society	88%
To improve corporate image	56%
To return part of profits to society	46%
To develop corporate morale	23%
Strong demand from outside	13%

Source White Paper *Corporate Philanthropy in Japan* (1992) Keidanren/Keizai, Koho Center.

But Japanese companies have had to learn that what works in Japan is not necessarily the most productive strategy in the USA. Accordingly, a number of Japanese corporations have shown a growing interest in relating their philanthropic efforts in the USA increasingly to strategic business concerns. The Matshushita Foundation (formed in 1984), for example, changed its name in the early 1990s to the Panasonic Foundation to obtain more direct identity of the corporate giving effort with the brand name, Panasonic, under which its products are marketed in the US. The Hitachi Group of Companies, through Hitachi Ltd, has chosen to keep the actions of the Hitachi Foundation separate from any direct business interest, but it engages in business-related philanthropic activity through the contributions of its main subsidiaries. Hitachi Maxell, which produces video and cassette tapes, participates in a cause-related marketing programme for Missing Children; a percentage of the price of each cassette or tape sold goes to this organization. Sony had done such a good job of projecting the company as American, not Japanese, that up until 1992 when Sony's founder, Akio Morita, openly complained about US society in league with a right-wing Japanese politician, most US citizens did not know it was a Japanese company. The work of the Sony Foundation USA was an active component of Sony's 'Americanization' strategy.

This does not amount to convergence, however. International corporations do not thus far appear to embrace to any significant extent the US corporate inclination to position CCI within a tighter strategic business framework. It can be argued that all international firms of whatever national origin encompass a degree of business interest in their CCI actions, not just in their US operations but elsewhere as well. However, there is little evidence that this 'degree' is affected appreciably by trends evident in the US. It must be remembered, too, that most US corporations make the majority of their philanthropic contributions within the US. As of 1995, only about $600 million (out of over $7 billion total corporate giving) found its way to locations and causes outside the US.

Is a business-related, self-interest CCI strategy counter-productive?

Most survey data show that it is US corporations that are most likely to ally their CCI actions with strategic business interests. While a sense of altruism continues to characterize some corporate giving programmes, most US companies engaged in philanthropy probably have a range of purposes, from the more social or altruistic to those more closely tied to business interest.

What do broad public surveys indicate about why companies do what they do? In the USA, 'the land of hype' as one European observer calls it, such survey data is readily available. In other parts of the world this is often not the case.

The 1995 *Yankelovich Monitor*, a public opinion poll data publication, indicates some rather interesting trends in views about the primary interests of US corporations. Table 4 presents a summary of the findings of this 1995 survey.

Between 1994 and 1995, there appears to have been a shift in public attitudes. There is a decline in the number reporting that business is 'concerned only with profits and not with the interests of the public' and also in the category 'business is concerned *mostly* [emphasis mine] with profits and not enough with the interests of the public'. In addition, with respect to business fairness and whether business is 'willing to give up some profits to put the interests of the public first', there is a change of public heart taking place.

Table 4 Summary judgement on business concerns

Agree more with:	1995 %	1994 %
Business is concerned only with profit and not with the interests of the public	14	16
or		
Business is concerned mostly with profits and not enough with the interests of the public	51	54
or		
Business tries to strike a fair balance between profits and the interests of the public	30	26
or		
Business is willing to give up some profits to put the interests of the public first	5	4

Source *Yankelovich Monitor*, 1995.

Over a longer time span, one sees a similar shift taking place. Table 5 addresses the public's view of American businesses' concern with 'making a profit' and 'other responsibilities'.

Table 5 Attitudes towards balance between profit and other responsibilities (%)

	1995 %	1994 %	1993 %	1992 %	1991 %	1990 %
American business is too concerned about making a profit and not concerned enough about its responsibilities to workers, consumers and the environment						
Total agree	**83**	**84**	**87**	**86**	**88**	**88**
Strongly agree	32	28	32	28	29	27
Agree	51	56	55	58	59	61
Total disagree	**17**	**16**	**13**	**14**	**12**	**12**
Disagree	16	15	12	13	11	11
Strongly disagree	1	1	1	1	1	1

Source *Yankelovich Monitor*, 1995.

Again, there is a steady decline in the number of Americans who believe that business is overly concerned with profits and insufficiently concerned about anything else.

It is noteworthy that this shift, albeit modest, is taking place at a time of considerable corporate downsizing and an increased corporate concern that community investments should reflect strategic business interests. One would have thought that the exact opposite would be reflected in the public's view, ie that business is concerned *more than ever* with the bottom line.

When reading such survey data one may wonder how aware the public is – in the USA or elsewhere – of the business practice called CCI. Corporate giving in the USA forms only a very small part of total US charitable giving, about $7.2 billion, or 3.6 per cent of the total $200 billion given in 1997. Not many American businesses make information about their giving actions publicly available. One might assume, therefore, that public views of business – for the most part – tend to be guided more by the market actions that a company takes than by what causes it funds.

There is, however, some indication that in the USA consumers may be more inclined to purchase the products of a company if they perceive that company as 'corporately responsible'. A 1994 study concluded that 'consumers had a greater attraction to doing business with companies regarded as doing something "good" for the community, as opposed to companies doing things detrimental to the community'.[6] Over 40 per cent of respondents indicated that their purchasing decisions were very much affected by the company's community-based programmes.

The bottom line on the 'bottom line'

As already noted, there is at least one form of convergence in CCI taking place. When a firm enters a foreign market, it may feel the need to conduct CCI activity *even when* there is no such requirement in the home market. This is why, for example, over 40 Japanese corporations have felt compelled to build foundations in the USA but only a few have done so in Western Europe or the Asia Pacific (excluding Japan). This is because it is expected that a foreign firm operating in the USA will be active in this way, and this isn't expected in Western Europe and the Asia Pacific, at least not to the same degree. Even US companies have only recently considered it necessary to carry the tradition of US corporate responsibility to foreign markets where they are operating.

Despite the limited convergence to date, I believe that the practice of linking CCI activities to business strategies will become more common, not less. Also, as noted earlier, I believe that this will enhance the quality of CCI practices and mutually benefit both companies and communities.

4 CCI worldwide: emerging themes and practices

As already stressed, I believe that every business seeks some form of advantage through its CCI programme. Even when more altruistic than business-minded, a company still hopes to be recognized for the contribution it has made. It wants to be considered a 'good citizen'.

The main objectives sought through CCI have already been detailed:

- demonstrating social responsibility;
- influencing the social and political environment in which the company operates;
- enhancing and protecting the company's reputation;
- improving employee morale;
- building business contacts and enhancing customer loyalty;
- on occasion, identifying product with the 'public good'.

With such objectives in mind, some businesses are adopting quite innovative approaches to designing their CCI programmes and projects. The Hitachi Group of Companies, through its US foundation, has emphasized the funding of under-served causes – multiculturalism and diversity in education, the environment, issues of importance to women and minorities, youth community service – since its inception in 1985. By taking on high-risk, unpopular causes, by definition receiving little or no support from philanthropic or indeed government organizations, and in most cases demonstrating that improvements can be forthcoming, Hitachi quickly became a recognized leader in CCI activities and the corporation soon saw that this was the best kind of self-interest. Less than 1 billion of the world's total population of almost 6 billion are now full participants in the modern global economy. If capitalism is to grow, then the other 5 billion have to be drawn in. Issues of poverty, job insecurity, racism, conflict resolution (there are over 200 armed conflicts of one sort or another under way as I write, mostly in impoverished countries), the environment, population growth, etc, are by far the 'toughest' issues here. I do not see how the private sector can continue to grow if it does not participate in finding solutions to these problems.

The Hitachi Foundation also chose to fund nationally rather than making community investments only where there are Hitachi facilities. Japanese firms such as NEC and Toshiba focus on funding for the disadvantaged; Panasonic negotiates compacts for school reform in selected US inner-city secondary school systems.

Some businesses are beginning to emphasize the need to have a positive and constructive influence on local, regional and national policy on such important issues as school-to-work transition, education reform, curriculum development in maths and science, and the environment. In 1995 the Switzerland-based World Business Council for Sustainable Development was formed to develop business policies and standards that effectively lead to the private sector contributing to sustainable development through sound environmental and resource management practices. It has a membership of 125 international companies drawn from 30 countries and more than 20 major industrial sectors.

In Europe the Hitachi Corporation and Canon are important contributors to an EU-wide review of state-sponsored job creation and job training capacities in direct response to the increasingly serious rise in unemployment, particularly in France. IBM provides equipment and software to the Australian Institute of Marine Science for conducting research on coral reef protection in the South-East Asian region. British Petroleum, through its Science Across Asia Pacific programme, links secondary school science students in 15 different countries in the region. By providing access to a database and educational materials on environmental topics, it gives students opportunities to exchange satellite-transmitted materials with counterparts in other countries and challenges them to consider the reasons for differences between countries in their approaches to environmental protection. Hongkong and Shanghai Bank, Cathay Pacific and the Caltex Companies (a Chevron Oil Company affiliate) provide support, corporate executive participation and technical expertise to the Hong Kong-based Private Sector Committee on the Environment, an organization that both reflects upon technical solutions to environmental impact problems and seeks to influence government policies on environmental clean-up and protection.

There is a growing trend in evidence worldwide – particularly among the industrialized nations – for companies to begin to use their internal research and development operations to provide solutions to community and social development problems. The Coca Cola Company, for example, uses its R&D operation to advise the emerging economies of Poland and Romania on the critical issues involved in the transition from an administered to a free-market operation. The Hitachi Corporation is making significant strides in developing technologies for the disadvantaged and seeks partnerships with educational institutions focusing on the hearing-, sight- and mobility-impaired to adapt these technologies to practical applications. Many companies are learning quickly that there is profit to be earned through bringing their R&D operations into direct contact with the task of seeking solutions to social problems and issues.

A company can choose to be benign in its practice of corporate citizenship, relying instead on the usual and somewhat static approaches to CCI. However, the dynamic company is learning that an increasingly innovative tack often leads to bottom-line benefits at the same time as improving the capacities of individuals and communities.

Themes of strategic corporate responsibility

Five broad themes underlying the alignment of CCI with business goals are set forth here. These themes are not meant to be all-inclusive, simply illustrative. The case studies that follow show the wide variety of motivations for and means to involving business self-interest 'strategically' in a company's CCI actions:

- protecting resource bases and gaining the licence to operate in new market areas;
- protecting and growing established, emerging and new markets, and market share;
- allying products with social causes and developing new products and marketing information through cause support and representation;
- building free-market operations capacity in emerging market economies and securing preferential treatment for products;
- gaining public and government acceptance of a foreign corporate presence.

I will examine each of these, citing actual cases of corporate action. It must be noted that the more innovative practitioners of CCI usually have more than one goal in any given CCI action. However, for purposes of illustrating each broad theme, in each case study I will focus on only one or two elements rather than all.

Protecting resource bases and gaining the licence to operate in new market areas

Case studies: Rio Tinto plc (UK); Atlantic Richfield Company (US); Aracruz Cellulose SA (Brazil)

Companies that are dependent upon raw materials are confronted with several major business challenges. They must gain the licence to operate in those parts of the world where the natural resources are located. Licence to operate is needed because extractive industries in particular pose serious threats and hazards to the environment. Companies in the extractive industries must therefore address adverse public opinion and must also be concerned with some form of equitable distribution of the gains from their exploitation of natural resources to the community at large.

Pharmaceutical and chemicals firms face different questions, though the latter clearly face challenges with respect to protecting the environment. Pharmaceutical companies often face charges of using countries in the developing world to test new unproven drugs and of developing drugs needed in poorer countries that those affected cannot possibly afford. In certain countries, particularly in Africa and South America, there are also special issues related to the licence to operate. Pharmaceutical and chemicals companies are increasingly concerned with access to plants indigenous to certain regions that may be or already are important to the development of pharmaceutical and bio-engineered products such as transgenics. In addition, new product development often depends on a licence to conduct field tests for specific adaptation of these new products.

RIO TINTO PLC (UK)

Rio Tinto plc (RT) is one of the world's leading metals and mining corporations. In 1997 its sales were $7.7 billion; it has more than 35,000 employees. Its main affiliate is Rio Tinto Ltd (Australia) and it has extensive operations in Africa, Latin America, the USA and the Asia Pacific.

RT's CCI programme travels under the banner 'The Global Neighbour'. Affiliated companies 'actively support local communities – both directly and through independently managed foundations – helping these communities adapt to the changes their [RT's subsidiaries and affiliates] operations can bring'. The firm's CCI programme focuses on education, the environment and community development – thereby addressing the three essential concerns of an extractive industry. RT's actions are not simply a matter of philanthropy. They are intended to maintain the licence to operate and continued access to raw materials: 'honouring responsibilities to employees and neighbours – playing an active role in the community – [is] *integral to the long-term well being of the business* [emphasis mine].'[7]

Specific actions to meet these business needs include:

■ The Palabora Foundation, the CCI arm of the Palabora Mining Company, operates in the Transvaal and focuses on self-development to 'ensure a growing pool of technically trained and educated people, competent managers and administrators in South Africa'. This work is tied to communities near the mine. There are also projects to upgrade school facilities and community infrastructure.

■ Similar projects in Namibia, Northern Zululand and Zimbabwe focus on technical education improvement, particularly the areas of skills and expertise needed in mining operations.

- Projects relating to diversification of community assets for broader sustainability in local economies are also undertaken. One of the most ambitious was undertaken by the Rio Tinto Zimbabwe Foundation in a community near Rio Tinto Zimbabwe's Renco mine. A dam was built that permitted an irrigation system to be developed. Ancillary small-scale industries, including fish farming, livestock breeding, orchards and tourism, also became feasible. Electrification, for both commercial and residential use, was an important by-product of this project.

RT effectively combines its business concerns – public acceptance for its presence and licence to operate; the need for a stream of qualified personnel; adequate community infrastructure to ensure healthy workers; broad public support and good relations with governments – with a contribution to the public good, particularly those parts of the public that reside near operating facilities.

ATLANTIC RICHFIELD COMPANY (US)

Atlantic Richfield Company (ARCO) is a global oil production and refining corporation, including petroleum and natural gas liquids. Mid-year 1998, it had $5.3 billion in sales; it has 24,000 employees.

ARCO's corporate responsibility programme, 'The Spirit of Giving', operates worldwide.[8] Tapping into oil and natural gas supplies, particularly in the Asia Pacific region, carries with it serious threats to the environment, especially to fragile coral reef formations and sea life habitats. In this region, the largest concentrations of population are found in the coastal areas. Accordingly, anything that may lead to coastal region degradation, endanger food supplies drawn from the sea, or pollute recreation and tourist areas must be serious concerns for a firm such as ARCO.

Like Rio Tinto, ARCO's CCI activities reflect these business concerns. Its project on Pagerungan Island in Indonesia reflects the company's version of 'good business equates with good citizenship'. ARCO has developed an offshore natural gas field that is the main source of Indonesia's natural gas requirements; the island has 4,000 inhabitants. ARCO's citizenship focus is the island population:

- In conjunction with the state-owned enterprise Pertamina and local community leaders, ARCO has developed a five-pronged community-based initiative reflecting ARCO's business concerns and the community's development needs. ARCO's aim was to protect the physical environment; contribute to and provide support for cultural and economic improvements; establish 'harmonious relations' with the islanders and the various local governments on the island; modernize the fishing industry, the primary source of income and food for island communities; and improve community social infrastructure – in education, health and culture.

■ ARCO has built four schools, housing for teachers and a Muslim school (Islam is the religion of the islanders). It has also renovated a mosque, built a village hall and a sports/youth centre and improved potable water production facilities. Health clinics and electric power generation facilities have been either constructed or improved.

■ ARCO's 'trenching, blasting, dredging and solid and liquid waste discharge from gas operations' are carried out according to an agreed environmental plan to reduce any negative impact on the environment.

■ An ice plant and cold storage facility have been constructed to enhance the basic livelihood of the islanders – fishing.

As ARCO developed the natural gas field, the construction equipment used could be used to construct and improve community facilities and infrastructure. Since the equipment had to be there anyway, the costs incurred in using it for community purposes was marginal.

Finding innovative ways to curb negative environmental impacts leads to important learning for the corporation that can be applied wherever it does business. Finally, recognizing that most of the islanders rely on fishing for their income and that in all probability few of the adults have any interest in working in ARCO production facilities, improving earning capacity necessrily meant improving the infrastructure of the main economic activity. Improved schools, as a long-term proposition, might well add an additional stream of qualified personnel for ARCO in the future.

The ARCO case demonstrates that business purpose, self-interest and improving the public good can travel compatibly together.

ARACRUZ CELLULOSE SA (BRAZIL)

Aracruz Cellulose operates timber plantations and a pulp production plant to supply paper manufacturers. It produces about 30 per cent of the world's bleached eucalyptus pulp and owns over 470,000 acres of tree plantations; the company is the largest landowner in Brazil.

From its inception as a company in 1967, Aracruz has pursued a policy of combining business goals with a comprehensive community investment and social improvement strategy. Rather than waiting to be forced by government regulation or public pressure to deal with such critical issues as environmental protection, poverty, ethnic diversity, and seriously limited social and community infrastructure, the company chose to develop its raw resource supply and product processing capacity in tandem with an action plan to improve the community and responsibly protect its raw materials resources. Thus, it anticipated the need to protect its licence to operate and its source of product inputs and to meet its human resource requirements by making the necessary community investments from the outset. Importantly, it built a base of sound relations and trust with local and national government officials and the public. As its CEO states, 'Business development is the major key to social progress.' He might well have added that social progress is the key to maintaining and protecting the right to develop business.

Actions that Aracruz has taken include:

- It has made a commitment to sustainable development by electing to be a founding member of the International Chamber of Commerce's Business Charter for Sustainable Development. It has also invested heavily in research on efficient management of forestry resources and improvement of seedlings, cutting growth time considerably.
- It leads the way in Brazil in conducting research on alternative wood construction materials, replacing rapidly depleting native species reserves with adapted eucalyptus varieties for housing and furniture, and as industrial fuel.
- It provides improved seedlings to local small farmers and foresters, both to reforest over-timbered lands and as a cash crop to improve income-earning capacity.
- It provides an enormous amount of support for improved community infrastructure, enabling major improvements in roads, housing, education, health and recreation facilities. It operates three training centres offering a rich choice of courses to both employees and other members of the community. It has built 14 public schools.[9]

The Aracruz example is illustrative of the benefits that can accrue from being strategic in serving business needs and community needs from the time analysis of investment feasibility is undertaken. This approach allows for collective business and community learning and thus for an integrated model of sustainable development where all parties can anticipate real returns. Maintaining a licence to operate and protecting raw resource material necessarily involves a community investment commitment. Aracruz recognizes that social progress is the price of doing business.

Protecting and growing established, emerging and new markets, and market share

Case studies: Microsoft Corporation (US); American Express Company (US)

There is some evidence that consumer loyalty is influenced by customer perception of the social responsibility of a company. In the USA annual surveys over the past decade have shown a steady rise in the number of respondents indicating that they are guided by this perception in their product purchases. There are of course many well-known cases of consumer boycotts. After the *Exxon Valdez* oil spill in Alaska, many motorists chose not to purchase gas from Exxon stations. More recently, Texaco was forced to make contributions to African American causes in the USA because of its discriminatory employment policies regarding employees. A major boycott of Texaco stations was narrowly avoided.

While this kind of consumer behaviour may not be widespread outside the USA, there is growing evidence that companies do run the risk of customer defections if they are caught in the act of unsound environmental practices. The case of Royal Dutch Shell Oil's plan to sink an obsolete oil production platform in the North Sea is but one example. As it turned out, the company's plan was the most sensible, but organizations such as Greenpeace and the European Green Party won the PR battle that ensued.

In many new and emerging markets, future and continued profitability depends upon firms building the necessary infrastructure to ensure a well-trained, productive workforce. Assigning people from the USA is both more costly than obtaining local workers and incurs public resentment. In addition, companies need to ensure that their employees have access to potable water, decent housing and health care, and education and training facilities. In China, for example, more often than not government officials demand that foreign investors take on such responsibilities as a condition of being allowed to operate at all. Even where a foreign presence is allowed by law, the public may nevertheless be opposed to its presence, and CCI activities can help the company win public support. It is not surprising, then, to find that companies are using their CCI activities to secure market acceptance, growth and sustainability.

MICROSOFT CORPORATION (US)

Microsoft Corporation is a leading software products and operating systems manufacturer. Sales for the first half of 1998 were $14.5 billion; it has more than 22,000 employees. It markets its products worldwide.

Computer technology is one of the most rapidly growing fields throughout the world. Shortages of trained, technically qualified personnel are reaching what can only be described as epic proportions in some countries. In this field, labour has a higher mobility than is the case in other occupations.

In Ireland Microsoft has developed the Microsoft European Scholar Programme called 'Tramlines'. The primary purpose of this programme, according to Microsoft, is to 'ensure that the benefits of the information age are fairly distributed'.[10]

- The programme is run in partnership with the Ballymun Job Centre; the target group is the urban-based, long-term unemployed. This target group typically has little work experience and, correspondingly, low self-esteem and confidence.
- The goal is to train the target group to 'become high-level computer professionals', qualified to receive the Microsoft Certified Professional (MCP) designation. In addition, the programme involves building knowledge of computer software, on-the-job training modules, personal development skill training (especially in communications, assertiveness training and detailed career analysis), business management training and community service.
- The training is intensive and demanding; over 70 per cent of the graduates have obtained full-time jobs, about one-third of these at Microsoft facilities.

While small scale – there have been only about 67 graduates – this approach is nevertheless strategic. It focuses on the hard-core, urban unemployed, and has registered a relatively high degree of success. It provides a small pool of locally trained talent for Microsoft operations and other IT firms – valuable both in terms of avoiding the high costs of importing personnel and in terms of winning public support in an area of high unemployment.

Its main accomplishment may well be the demonstration that, given the right commitment by both company and target group, in-roads can be made even in the case of the hard-core unemployed. Companies considering overseas investments are inevitably drawn to situations where qualified technicians are available. Ireland's economic future is at least partially dependent upon its ability to make such talent available.

There is another self-interest issue served in Microsoft's action. Software firms are losing billions of dollars worldwide to product pirating. If this illegal activity is to be curbed, companies like Microsoft are going to need good relations with the governments of countries where this activity prospers. Assisting the government in dealing with serious and often intractable employment problems, even in a small way, can have long-term benefits in this respect.

AMERICAN EXPRESS COMPANY (US)

American Express (AMEX) is a diversified financial services, travel and tourism corporation. In 1998 its sales were $18.5 billion; it has more than 73,000 employees worldwide and offices in every country in the world.

Focusing on the travel/tourism line of business, it is clear that the company has a strong vested interest in the development of tourism and tourist facilities. Given the rapid growth of Asian markets, characterized by rapidly increasing individual incomes, the corporation has been particularly interested in the Asian market potential.

Tourism has been and remains one of the mainstays of most emerging economies. A goal of the American Express Company is to protect natural and manmade tourist resources. Given the conflicts that have ravaged the Asia Pacific region, for example in Cambodia, Laos and Vietnam, the company has, through its American Express Foundation, taken a two-pronged approach to protecting and enhancing market potential for future tourism growth. AMEX employee involvement and grants are being directed to:

■ a public information campaign on the need for historic and environmental preservation, and on the kinds of government policies needed to protect valuable cultural, religious and historical sites;
■ supporting important institutions – museums, cultural preservation organizations and related government ministries – and major projects in the visual and performing arts dedicated to preserving cultures throughout the Asia Pacific region.

Actions include:

■ collaborating with all parties that have a vested interest in cultural and historic preservation, including industry associations, national governments and community groups;
■ funding a number of important small and large-scale projects, such as restoring the Hindu-Buddhist Site at Anghor Wat, Cambodia (with a team comprised of World Monuments Fund, UNESCO and Japanese experts); restoring the Temple of Literature in Vietnam (with the Vietnam Ministry of Culture and Information); supporting World Monuments Watch, in conjunction with the World Monuments Fund, in an effort to raise public awareness of the need to identify, preserve and protect important cultural and historic sites worldwide.

The business rationale for AMEX undertaking this effort is clear: sound preservation leads to a growing market for AMEX products and services. By helping to preserve important historical and religious sites, the company adds to the capital assets upon which the tourist industry and its revenues depend. The public is also well served: as a result of this effort, important religious and cultural artefacts stand a better chance of surviving.

Allying products with social causes and developing new products and marketing information through cause support and representation

Case studies: Timberland Company (US); Monsanto Corporation (US); British Petroleum plc (UK); Ciba-Geigy (SW)

Cause-related marketing is assumed to have begun when the American Express Company acted to support the renovation of the Statue of Liberty in the late 1970s, linking use of its charge cards to generating the funds needed for the project. Since then many corporations have allied with causes, though without necessarily linking product sales to the exercise. Pharmaceutical companies are particularly active in social marketing. Other types of firm support a broad range of issues: breast cancer, literacy, AIDS, drug and substance abuse, teenage pregnancy, the homeless and the hungry.

One of the best known is Merck & Company's decision to donate a drug for prevention of river blindness to the World Health Organization. Merck's business interest here was to avoid the criticism that surely would have come if it did nothing with the river blindness drug it had developed. The nations where this disease is rampant are largely poor, so trying to sell it at any meaningful return would have engendered a serious and negative public reaction.

A somewhat similar approach is being used by Ciba-Geigy. It has worked to develop treatments and facilities for leprosy patients and pro-grammes of early detection, and it has also undertaken awareness campaigns to deal with the social stigma attached to leprosy. This is a busi-ness approach designed to help Ciba identify care approaches and possibly lead to new product R&D situations – and is just possibly a stroke of genius. Through an entrepreneurial business approach you 'mainstream' a disease with an enormous social stigma attached to it as a means of mak-ing the public more aware and informed of the need for cures and care and presumably beginning to break down the social barriers that currently prevent adequate treatment.

This approach goes beyond the tying of product sales to cause support and has become known as 'social marketing', where the company name becomes closely associated with the 'good' cause.

The business purpose dimension is undergoing further mutation as companies learn that alliance with a cause can lead to new product ideas and marketing information, generated from public response to cause awareness. Nowhere is this more apparent than in the area of environ-mental protection awareness. The number of 'green' products, not to mention the number of business councils formed that focus on environmental protection and needed industry response, has risen geometrically in the past 15 years.

THE TIMBERLAND COMPANY (US)

The Timberland Company is a footwear and clothing manufacturer. In 1998 its sales were more than $820 million. It has 5,100 employees and markets its products both in the USA and internationally.

The company has no formal CCI function in its organizational structure – there is no corporate foundation or direct corporate contributions office. Annually, it gives its employees 40 hours of paid time off to volunteer in the community. It has a recycling programme, and is considered a leading smaller company in the practice of good corporate citizenship.

One of the social causes with which the company allies itself is drug abuse. Its approach has been most innovative:

- It has developed a 'Give the Boot to Drugs' initiative. Posters were printed, the central feature of which is a Timberland boot; these posters advocate support for local and national efforts to do away with drug use and expand drug treatment facilities. It also produced a video on the same theme. Both posters and videos have been popular in Timberland's foreign markets, particularly in Italy.
- The company also markets cause-advocacy clothing in its retail outlets. Part of the proceeds of the sales go to support various drug abuse prevention and treatment organizations.
- Employees are encouraged to volunteer for organizations that combat the use of drugs.

What is particularly interesting about the Timberland case is that, early on, it realized that its cause-related wear was not selling well and so not generating substantial funds. An enterprising company executive began to apply basic marketing principles – the same principles applied to marketing Timberland's main clothing and footwear lines – to resolve the problem. Clothes shops are laid out to attract customers and affect buying decisions. It was discovered that the cause-related wear often occupied the least desirable display space. He convinced the marketing department to remedy this and place displays closer to the store entrance. The result? Not only did sales skyrocket but sales of the Timberland-brand wear improved markedly also, often by as much as 20 per cent. This business-like approach served both the cause and the business interest simultaneously, in that the cause-related effort generated important marketing information that was beneficial to the business through increased sales and beneficial to the cause through increased donations.

Timberland does not as a matter of course seek bottom-line business benefit in the social issues it undertakes to support, but it now knows that this is possible. Ironically, if the company had been looking for increased sales, and if the Vice President of Marketing had been less enterprising, then Timberland would have taken the anti-drug abuse wear off the shelves and sought a different and possibly more saleable cause-wear, and that would have been the end of it.

MONSANTO COMPANY (US)

Monsanto is a diversified chemical, pharmaceutical, agricultural product and food ingredients manufacturer. In 1997 its sales were $9.5 billion; it has 21,900 employees. The company markets its products worldwide. It is engaged in agri-biotechnology research, seeking to identify improved varieties of foodstuffs and crops that are disease-resistant.

Projections of population growth place the world total at somewhere between 8 and 10 billion by the year 2025. World hunger is a serious issue. Those tracking the environmental problems of the earth argue that the capacity to produce ever-larger crop yields is waning. Massive food shortages might be overcome through technology breakthroughs.

At the present time, the 15 or so public agricultural research centres located mostly in developing countries receive very little funding for agri-biotechnology research. In 1993, for example, the total budget of these centres for this kind of research equalled about 10 per cent of Monsanto's for similar research; Monsanto is a medium-sized firm. The reality is that most promising agri-biotechnologies are proprietarily held by the private sector.

Monsanto, with additional support from the Hitachi and Rockefeller Foundations, supported the establishment of a new service that could broker the transfer of promising agri-biotechnologies from the private to the public sector. This project is rather more complex than one usually finds in cause-related funding, but it does demonstrate the power of innovation and partnership.

■ The Hitachi Foundation (formed by Hitachi Ltd) took the lead in funding the initial work of the new organization, the International Service for the Acquisition of Agri-Biotech Applications (ISAAA), now domiciled at Cornell University.

■ Once established, ISAAA concluded an arrangement for the transfer of a transgenic, in this case a potato virus developed by Monsanto, by donating it to Mexico. Potatoes in Mexico are a mainstay of the population's diet, and more than 25 per cent of the crop was being lost to diseases. In addition, the need for large quantities of fertilizers and pesticides was straining Mexico's balance of payments and foreign currency reserves, not to mention the severe environmental hazards resulting from their use.

■ Upon donating the virus, the Rockefeller Foundation provided a large grant to support the indigenous research establishment in Mexico to work closely with Monsanto in field-testing and adapting the potato virus to local conditions. This was to ensure the full development of a disease-resistant strain and also, simultaneously, to build Mexico's research capability rather than have Mexico forever dependent on outside research assistance.

Mexico's success with this project is impressive; it has already commercialized three transgenic products, and it is the first developing country to field-test a transgenic virus-resistant potato developed by its own national scientists.

Monsanto's self-interest is clear. Although its action would reduce the demand for some of its products – fertilizers and pesticides – newer products come on line that often have stronger market potential than traditional ones. Although somewhat controversial, the company, like most of those working on transgenics, must have opportunities to field-test these under differing environmental and geographical circumstances. This project – a cooperation between a major corporation, a medium-sized Japanese private corporate foundation and a large US private foundation – has demonstrated that a transfer on a donated basis makes sense when it is designed to create not new dependencies for developing countries but indigenous capacity in bio-technologies.

BRITISH PETROLEUM PLC (UK)

British Petroleum plc (BP) is one of the world's largest petroleum producing and refining companies. In 1997 company sales were more than $71 billion. It has more than 56,000 employees; it produces and markets its products worldwide.

BP is a leader in supporting cause-related projects around the globe. One problem BP chooses to address is urban and rural health care in South Africa.[11]

■ The company, in conjunction with the ANC, UNICEF, the European Union and a variety of local organizations of health-care professionals and community workers, used modern multimedia technologies to improve public awareness of the issues.

■ Because soap operas are so popular in many developing regions, the primary medium used was a TV series called *Soul City*. A 'squatter camp' was the venue for a 13-part series broadcast in English and Zulu and presented at peak TV watching hours. The series dramatized critical health issues such as safe child-rearing and mothering skills, the need for immunizations, malnutrition, child abuse, and good health practices.

- Other media were also used. As a companion piece to *Soul City*, a 60-part radio series entitled *Healing Hearts* was broadcast in three languages (Zulu, Xhosa and Sotho). Press campaigns and education materials dissemination were also conducted.

Between the two series, an estimated 14 million South Africans were reached. The programme is being packaged for other African audiences and the multimedia materials repackaged for schools and for health and community workers. From a business interest standpoint, this project has had some impact. The educational booklet that accompanied the *Soul City* series was distributed through BP service stations and other outlets. The primary business benefit was being allied with such a significant social cause and an innovative approach.

CIBA-GEIGY CORPORATION (SWITZERLAND)

Ciba-Geigy is a major chemical and pharmaceuticals manufacturer. The company has a long tradition of CCI. It has supported a number of specific causes, such as leprosy, and more general sustainable community development, particularly in developing countries. Through one of its innovations, a corporate 'Risk Fund', it encourages its affiliates in developing countries 'to take up innovative, commercially oriented projects, even if they entail long start-up periods, high pre-investments and costly project supervision'.[12]

The project is first and foremost a business project: the Fund is to 'help improve the long-term commercial success of the divisions'. It does not preclude pursuit of the commercial development of products and services that might come out of 'cause-related' initiatives financed through Fund activity. Unlike other causes the company supports, Risk Fund projects must be commercially viable and entrepreneurially based.

- A decision was made to use Risk Fund resources in a four-country pilot study (Egypt, Ecuador, Indonesia and Kenya) to increase public awareness of the causes of epilepsy and to change public behaviour towards those with this affliction. The approach was essentially one of social marketing. At its commercial core, the pilot projects were intended to expand the use and market for Ciba's epilepsy treatment drug, Tegretol.
- The pilot project provided training seminars and workshops to improve diagnosis and treatment of the disease. This training reached a large number of doctors and health-care staff in all four countries.
- An information campaign was conducted to improve public attitudes towards those with the disease. In three of the countries, television was used.

This approach clearly proves that the private sector has a great deal to bring to the resolution of social concerns in the way of marketing, public relations, advertising and training expertise gained in competitive circumstances. While social good and profitability are combined in this approach, the return to the company is the predominant concern in applying Risk Fund resources to the causes of, and treatment for, epilepsy. The public information campaign, in changing attitudes and behaviour to those afflicted, is a reasonable 'public good', as is advancing the knowledge and diagnostic and treatment capabilities of doctors and other health-care professionals.

Building free-market operations capacity in emerging market economies and securing preferential treatment for products

Case studies: The Coca Cola Company (US); Nestlé (Thailand) Ltd (Switzerland)

Since the late 1980s, over 2.4 billion people, previously living in the administered economies of centrally planned, communist-dominated countries, now find themselves in free-market regimes. Former Soviet Union and Eastern Bloc countries are the most prominent examples, but there are many others with a history of central economic and social planning and administration, including Egypt, India and China (although the last is still a communist country).

One of the interesting questions facing foreign corporations that wish to invest in these newly liberalized economies is the extent to which they have to provide assistance in the overall transition to a market economy in order to realize the profits from market opportunities there? It is often difficult to realize market potential simply because there is insufficient market infrastructure; no one knows the rules, and governments are often ill equipped to enforce rules even if they do exist.

A slightly different issue is the extending of free-market growth to those living in rural areas in emerging economies. Often rural areas neither participate in nor benefit from the growth of free-market activity. This can even lead to dissident movements hosting elements intent on overthrowing the government regime. While there are limits to what any company will be willing to do to provide resources to rural areas, there are clear risks in such important market areas as Indonesia, China, Mexico and India in failing to address the needs of rural populations.

THE COCA COLA COMPANY (US)

Coca Cola is a soft-drinks manufacturer with widely diversified food processing and agricultural production holdings. In 1997 its sales were over $18 billion. It has 29,500 employees and licenses bottlers and distributors worldwide.

The Coca Cola Company was one of the first to move into markets of the former Soviet Union and the former Eastern Bloc. The development of the company's business in Romania illustrates the way in which a private foreign corporation, through its business arm and its foundation, can assist the economic transition and secure a market share for its products.[13]

■ Through establishing bottling operations, and linkages with the relatively small retail sector, which sold high turnover products such as soft drinks and tobacco, Coca Cola helped stimulate an economic transition. The company triggered a retail boom, mostly because the availability of a Western product served to draw consumers to the small retail kiosks.

■ This forward market linkage helped to create a new entrepreneurial class. By the mid-1990s, the number of small retail kiosks had increased from a few thousand to almost 30,000, supporting an estimated 25,000 jobs. The company also provided important business management skills.

■ While the indicators do not show that Coca Cola triggered other foreign investment, it nevertheless contributed significantly and early on to the re-emergence of an entrepreneurial class, which is an important building block for future free-market development.

■ By introducing modern standards of production, marketing and management, the company demonstrated that quality production and marketing were obtainable locally. The company, in effect, played the role of a 'flagship' for positive action in a difficult economic transition.

■ The company sponsored sports and arts events, neither of which could any longer be supported by the state, the express purpose being to advertise company products. Sponsorship is thus part of the total package that has led to Coca Cola's dominant position in the Romanian soft-drinks market.

The effects of Coca Cola's entry into the Romanian market were perhaps more valuable symbolically than in terms of magnitude. A major foreign multinational entered a very difficult political and economic situation, thus lending credibility to the notion that a relatively underdeveloped economy could sustain and make profitable a foreign economic presence. Through support of local business development, and assisting in the formation of entrepreneurial talent, Coca Cola's presence and product symbolized the country's nascent effort to modernize the economy and the society. Its market share and dominance could only increase.

NESTLÉ (THAILAND) LTD

The Nestlé Corporation, a Swiss company, is the world's largest food manufacturer. In 1997 its sales were $70 billion. The company's production facilities are located throughout the world and it markets its products globally.

The rural areas of Thailand have been largely untouched by the economic growth found in Bangkok. Thai farmers' income is about US$16–$24 a month, although they can increase this by working as unskilled labourers in Bangkok where monthly wages are $60–$80. Most farmers spend about half the year away from the village and their family. Those left behind fend for themselves as they can.

Nestlé (Thailand) Ltd, a subsidiary of the giant Swiss firm Nestlé SA, began experimenting with a community development loan fund in 1993. In conjunction with the Thai Business Initiative in Rural Development (TBIRD), a revolving loan fund was created to lend money to villagers at reasonable rates.

- Villagers pay a small fee to join the fund and another small annual fee plus a monthly interest rate of 2 per cent. Loans are given for small-scale enterprises such as repair services, weaving, and poultry and crop raising. Repayment schedules depend upon the nature of the enterprise.
- Applicants for funds must be backed by five to seven of their peers who act to guarantee the loan. A management committee is formed from members of the fund, who receive a two-day course in village fund management.

After three years of the project, the fund size had increased by 20 per cent. Fund managers, drawn from the community, had learned a great deal about what kinds of enterprise work and how the village can better shape its development. Borrowers who have been successful are able to enjoy financial security for the first time in their lives: several of the projects increased income by 30–70 per cent. There have been no defaults on the loans.

The company did not seek any particular business advantage from the project. However, Nestlé (Thailand) uses a large number of small-scale business and agricultural projects to augment its supplier base. Such arrangements are usually stipulated in foreign investment agreements reached with host governments requiring outsourcing from local businesses. The success of the projects allows the company to diversify its supplier base so that a greater part of the population benefits. In Thailand it has thousands of small suppliers, a number of which have been supported by the company's rural community development effort. It also allows the company to fulfil its agreed obligations to support local business and community development.

Nestlé had tried similar projects in Thailand with other organizations but without much success. By entering this project with TBIRD, the company was able to draw on the considerable experience of this intermediary organization in successful community development. While such projects may provide only incremental benefits to Nestlé, the government has a vested interest in maintaining stability in rural areas.

Gaining public and government acceptance of a foreign corporate presence

Case studies: Hitachi Ltd and Hitachi America Ltd (Japan); Grand Metropolitan plc (UK)

Often companies do not experience difficulty in entering a foreign market *per se*. Laws permit such investment, although in some countries these laws and attending regulations are quite prohibitive. In emerging markets, for example in Egypt, China, Mexico and India, the bureaucratic maze through which a prospective foreign (and, on occasion, domestic) private investor must pass to gain permission to establish a business presence is, to say the least, daunting.

There is potentially a different order of magnitude of difficulty for a foreign company in gaining public acceptance in the new country, even if government approval is given for an investment. Currently, while huge amounts of foreign investment are flooding into the newly emerging markets, particularly in Asia, the largest capital flows pass between the industrialized countries/regions: Japan, the USA and Western Europe. The UK is the heaviest investor in the USA, followed by Japan, Germany and the Netherlands. Canada is the USA's largest trading partner; Mexico is the second largest. The USA and Western European countries relentlessly chip away at the barriers to foreign investment in Japan; the USA is a major foreign investor in the UK, Germany and France; so is Japan.

Despite any government's agreement to a foreign investor presence, companies often still have to earn public acceptance for this presence. Politicians quickly agree to impose restrictions if public resentment or xenophobia becomes substantial. This is as true in industrialized countries as in developing countries.

The cases in this category, one Japanese firm and one from the UK, illustrate the particular problems each encountered in entering the US market as an investor. British firms have a long history of investing in the USA, while Japanese investment there is far more recent. Because the USA is largely Anglophile and certainly Europhile, there has not been broad antagonism towards UK firms, but the same cannot be said for Japanese corporations. Yet, if a company makes a mistake at the local level – where a foreign company's presence is most conspicuous – there can be negative consequences. These cases demonstrate how two firms had to respond, in their 'self-interest', to negative attitudes on the part of the public.

HITACHI LTD AND HITACHI AMERICA LTD (JAPAN)

Hitachi Ltd is a manufacturer of electronics and electrical equipment. With over 20,000 different products, it is the most diversified of all major Japanese corporations. In 1997 the company's sales were $68.5 billion. It has more than 330,000 employees worldwide. Hitachi America Ltd (HAL) is Hitachi Ltd's wholly owned US subsidiary. HAL accounts for about $5–$7 billion of Hitachi's total sales.

For most major Japanese corporations, true globalization did not begin until the early 1980s. Up to that point, most of them operated highly sophisticated trading organizations, rather than an offshore plant presence, to conduct their international business.

The economic rationale for establishing offshore plant, service, R&D and general administrative operations is rooted in the volume of exports to a particular market. There is a point when the export market in a particular country or region is sufficiently large to merit major capital and plant investments to serve it. There are of course other reasons: wage differentials (between home country and foreign markets); foreign market political resistance to further imports rather than capital investment in their country; the need to have on-the-ground marketing, advertising, packaging and R&D knowledge to grow markets at the margin and remain competitive, and to have executive and production talent well schooled in operating in national and business cultures other than their own.

Both a favourable exchange rate and the Reagan administration's pressure on Japanese companies to invest directly in the USA drove Japanese corporations to increase direct investments in the US. In 1985 Hitachi Ltd and its wholly owned subsidiary, Hitachi America Ltd, committed themselves to do three things:

- increase direct investment in the US market (in 1985 Hitachi employed about 4,000 US employees and operated about 35 facilities);
- increase by $1 billion their purchase of US-produced capital and intermediate capital goods, to be used in Japan-based production of Hitachi products;
- create a corporate foundation (with an initial endowment of $20 million and a further $20 million over the next ten years. The Foundation also directly influenced about $1–$4 million per year in direct Hitachi contributions in the USA for disasters such as the San Francisco earthquake and various hurricanes).

By 1997 Hitachi had over 20,000 US employees in over 180 facilities, and sales had increased from about $2 billion to over $5 billion. Hitachi Ltd and HAL were but one Japanese corporation among the many that had established a foundation and/or a direct corporate giving function since 1985.

Hitachi's 'good corporate citizenship' drive focused on establishment of the Hitachi Foundation.

▪ While the Foundation was to be a private corporate foundation, governed by a board drawn from prominent American leaders, it was given the Hitachi name. The corporation did not wish to be seen to control the Foundation's actions, but giving it the name of its benefactor was a major act of trust: a Japanese corporation's name, and correspondingly its reputation, is everything.

▪ The senior leadership of the Foundation made the decision to address under-served causes in the USA, not, as would be charged later, 'to curry favour with US minority groups for political advantage' but because it was thought that through this work the Foundation would be focusing on what it anticipated were the toughest issues US society and its business sector would face, and at the same time would quickly become a recognized leader in CCI activities.

▪ Although not part of the company, the senior leadership of the Foundation sought, nevertheless, to build an active partnership with its benefactor. It was felt that the real learning regarding citizenship would need to reside with those staffing the many corporate facilities around the country, not just with the professional staff of the Foundation.

▪ This partnership was built on two main programmes. The first was a matching funds scheme between participating Hitachi facilities and the Foundation, which created a pool of funds to support local community investments. Decisions as to causes, projects and organizations supported would be made by community action committees made up of employees (both Japanese and American). The second programme supported youth service to the community. The Yoshiyama Award for Exemplary Community Service recognizes young Americans for their independent and entrepreneurial actions to solve community issues and problems. Several corporate employees help screen candidates for this award.

The purpose of the Foundation was to provide important learning to the corporation and to its executives and employees as they built the Hitachi presence in communities around the US. The Foundation did not tie its funding only to plant locations. It was believed that the task of building Hitachi's reputation as a corporate citizen was a national – indeed, a global (Japanese corporations don't have a public acceptance problem only in the USA) – undertaking.

Was there business self-interest involved in creating the Foundation and in its subsequent operations? Yes; changing Hitachi's image in a critical market was an important goal – and in doing this it demonstrated that sound, relevant community investments, rather than PR 'spin' approaches, are the most effective way to improve a company's image as a 'good corporate citizen'. The

Hitachi Group of Companies is a world-class business; the Foundation aimed to make it a world-class corporate citizen as well. By 1993 the CCI activities of Hitachi and other Japanese corporations had brought resources totalling almost $400 million to hundreds of different US causes, educational institutions and non-profit organizations – roughly the same amount as was given by all US corporations to causes and non-profits outside the US.

GRAND METROPOLITAN PLC (UK)
(now part of DIAGEO PLC)

Grand Metropolitan plc (GrandMet) was a packaged food and beverage producer and operated retail food outlets. In 1997 its sales were over $14 billion. It had substantial investments in the USA and the European Union.

Foreign investment in the USA by UK firms remains larger than investments by firms of other nations. When Grand Metropolitan found itself in difficulty in the USA, it was not due to its British origin. The problem was that it was seen, at least initially, to be ready to diminish the community commitment of one of the icons and leaders of corporate responsibility, the Pillsbury Company (which it was purchasing).

- GrandMet conducted a hostile takeover of the Pillsbury Company in 1989. Pillsbury was an old-line company in the Minneapolis–St Paul community, formed in 1869. The Pillsbury Foundation was considered an important leader in the community; it was also considered one of the best US corporate foundations.
- In response to the proposed takeover, a rally staged by community organizations and non-profit organizations raised questions about GrandMet's corporate citizenship and whether the present giving of Pillsbury – $8 million – would be in jeopardy.
- GrandMet appeared to be ready to downscale the giving effort – something that another British firm, BP, would be charged with in Cleveland, Ohio, after its purchase of SOHIO – and subsequent changes in the leadership of the Pillsbury Foundation underscored this concern.
- There was open public hostility to the takeover. GrandMet made no effort during the takeover to assuage public concern, even though it had an active CCI agenda in the UK and in other countries where it had operations.

In response to the criticism and suspicion, GrandMet agreed to maintain the size of the giving programme – although it made no commitment to continue to concentrate that giving in the Minneapolis–St Paul area. It also pledged to remain a member of the Keystone Club, a local group of businesses pledged to commit between 2 and 5 per cent of pre-tax profits to community causes.

These commitments by GrandMet assuaged public concerns somewhat. However, the company radically changed the character of the former Pillsbury Foundation giving programme. Cause-related marketing is now the mainstay of its corporate giving, and programmes are conducted in the over 30 US communities where the company has plant locations. As is noted in GrandMet's *Report on Corporate Citizenship* (1997), '[GrandMet] wanted to extend Pillsbury's reputation as a good corporate citizen over a wider geographical area and to involve other parts of the company and their retailer customers in community work.' This goal is more consistent with GrandMet's efforts to be strategic in its CCI activities, and can clearly be interpreted as being more in GrandMet's self-interest.

5 Good corporate citizenship: the broader picture

Good corporate citizenship practice cannot overcome the effects of poor business ethics and bad business decisions. However, a company's reputation for good citizenship can mitigate adverse public opinion, depending upon what precipitated this.

Companies must also be careful not to make unwarranted claims about the impact they have had in supporting a community cause. The most ardent advocates of serving business needs through a company's CCI programme realize how difficult it is to quantify the effect these programmes have. Hence, good citizenship, whether self-interested or purely altruistic, is not a panacea. Simply linking the company's business self-interest to CCI activity does not mean that this self-interest will always be served.

The question remains: how do we wish our private businesses to be involved as 'good' citizens in the broader community – however this community is defined?

Corporate responsibility – a Catch-22

The answer to this question is elusive. A company might define an approach to a community issue that simultaneously serves its strategic business self-interest, only to find that it has miscalculated. The public can be quite fickle in according its favour to corporations' CCI practices.

A most interesting case that arose in 1997 illustrates the occasional ironies involved in being corporately responsible.

PHILLIPS-VAN HEUSEN CORPORATION (US)

Phillips-Van Heusen (PVH) is a vertically integrated manufacturer, marketer and retailer of men's, women's and children's clothing and footwear. Its 1997 sales were $1.36 billion; it has 8,450 employees. Like many clothing manufacturers, PVH produces most of its clothing in low-wage countries in Latin America and Asia.

The company's CEO, Bruce Klatsky, is a 'champion of civil rights' (*Wall Street Journal*, 2 February 1997). He sits on the Human Rights Watch board and a White House committee seeking to end abuses in the needle trades and footwear manufacturing. The company has a tough code of conduct, the main elements of which include:

- treating employees fairly with regard to wages, benefits and working conditions;
- never violating the legal or moral rights of employees in any way;
- never employing children in its facilities or doing business with any company that uses child labour.

The code goes on to state: 'Phillips-Van Heusen is committed to an ongoing programme of monitoring all our facilities and those of companies with whom we do business.' This is the kind of corporate statement that critics of private business say is necessary. And, in fact, Mr Klatsky apparently follows up on these words with deeds.

A controversy arose when a civil rights activist group reported that PVH, in its Guatemalan plants, was '[paying] wages below poverty levels, [hiring] contractors [using] underage employees and [intimidating] union organizers' – although Mr Klatsky's critics do not dispute the fact that the company has worked hard to improve working conditions, which are well above standard when compared to other factories in the country. It has introduced subsidized lunches, free on-site health care and school supplies for employees' children. Ergonomic chairs are provided for sewing workers, and the wages paid are 'higher' than for other similar jobs in Guatemala. In addition, through its CCI programme, ' the company has contributed more than $1.5 million to improve nutrition, facilities and teacher education at schools in the village where many PVH contractors work'.

The message here is that there appears to be a desire to achieve very high standards – almost perfection. But why aren't a company's serious and best efforts to effect social improvements at the very least credit-worthy, particularly within the competitive context in which a private business works and must survive? What other type of organization do we hold to such lofty standards?

A postscript to the PVH case is also illustrative. In March 1997, the US Department of Labor added the company to the Trendsetters' List – those garment retailers and manufacturers that take additional steps to ensure that their goods are not made in sweatshop conditions. The Secretary of Labor noted: 'The difference between following trends and setting them comes down to doing what is right.'

On 16 April 1997, workers at PVH's Guatemalan plant achieved union recognition. The company's 'change of heart' occurred after Mr Klatsky read a Human Rights Watch report that described the anti-union discrimination and intimidation of trade unionists by the firm's managers. 'Bruce Klatsky … an ardent defender of human rights, made it his personal responsibility to ensure greater respect of trade union rights,' noted the International Confederation of Free Trade Unions.

This case, and the CEO's response to the circumstances that evolved, indicate that while soundly conceived and serious CCI programmes can make an impact on social issues, business practices – and positive changes therein – can often have a much greater impact. However, good business practices do not obviate the need for CCI, nor can excellence in results achieved through CCI programmes obviate the need for improvements in business practices.

The CEO of Levi-Strauss & Co, Robert Haas, is recognized worldwide as one of the most articulate spokesmen on corporate responsibility. Under his direction, the company has refused to build plants in China because of the country's poor human rights conditions. The President of the United States, in an attempt to preserve long-term business interests in China, has been forced to turn somewhat of a blind eye to the human rights issue. Mr Haas's decision is all the more significant given the broader US corporate sentiment that led to the President's stand on the matter.

But Levi's is having business difficulties, and shareholders are pressuring the company to recant, or at least somewhat modify, Haas's stand. How perfect, or close to perfect, a citizen does a company have to be?

Even in the cases presented in Chapter 3, which cite CCI programmes thought to be innovative and benefiting both business and the community, one finds that other aspects of firms' behaviour may be criticized. Aracruz Cellulose SA, for example, has recently been charged with illegally making use of 13,000 hectares (about 33,000 acres) of 'land that rightfully belongs to the Tupinikim and Guarani indigenous peoples'. It will be recalled that Aracruz is providing social services and medical assistance to both the Tupinikim and the Guarani tribes. The fact that the company is supporting these services does not negate the charge, nor does the charge being made necessarily seem to be undermining Aracruz's effort to appear corporately responsible.

In the case of the Monsanto Corporation, multiple claims of irresponsibility have been made by the company's detractors. It has been criticized for the production of NutraSweet (an artificial sweetener), the genetically engineered BGH (bovine growth hormone) and – in what can only be described as one of the more bizarre claims – genetically engineered soya beans that are resistant to the company's chemical herbicide product, RoundUp. The implication of the last is that Monsanto ensures larger sales of the herbicide by developing strains of soya bean that have been designed to withstand the product's application.

What *can* the private business sector offer in the way of social improvements?

This question is rather fundamental, for if we cannot answer it other than ambiguously – in the most general of terms – then there will be no public consensus on the standards to which businesses must be held.

What does the private business sector do well, and is the expertise businesses gain relevant to efforts to improve the public good? Many now argue that the private sector is the most dynamic of the three sectors: government, private and non-profit. Companies that survive are effective organizers and managers; their firms adapt human, financial and technological resources to productive ends; they know how to communicate, package and market; they invest heavily in the development of new products and the R&D necessary for new product breakthroughs; and they do all this as efficiently and cheaply as possible.

What are the usual complaints about government-led efforts to improve the public good? These efforts are usually deemed wasteful, overly bureaucratic and too general in scope; and those engaged in them are not accountable for results. Does this lead us to the conclusion that while business cannot bring scale to social infrastructure improvement, it can bring ideas and new thinking, and perhaps a higher degree of efficiency and effectiveness? If so, one must consider whether the best way to accomplish this is for a company to be strategic in its approach, and to conduct its contribution to social improvements within the context which it knows best, which, as Chris Marsden puts it, is 'within the grain of business'.

Two things happen when a company is successfully able to link its corporate responsibility to its business goals:

- It is more likely to take its CCI activity seriously.
- It is more likely that the entire business organization will become involved, not just that part of the organization that is charged with administering the company's CCI programme. Achieving business goals calls for teamwork, systems, cooperation and coordinated planning.

Why are these things 'more likely'? For any company, the degree to which it brings real professionalism to its CCI programmes depends partly on the quality of management decision-making in the pursuit of profit. Even the best CCI programme won't survive if the company is going broke.

I contend that many companies do improve their performance on social goals when these goals are integral to achieving their business aims. Chapter 3 presents a number of such examples.

The limitations of corporate responsibility

It would be a mistake to assume that the private sector is experienced or particularly well suited to undertake all manner and form of community and social improvement.

The best companies practising sound CCI programmes recognize the limitations that attach to their role as good citizens. The scale of public needs and the need for improved social and economic infrastructure are well beyond the means available to any single corporation, or even a number of corporations acting in concert on any given issue. It is, however, useful to encourage corporations to use their entrepreneurial and innovative talents to assist communities and governments in finding solutions to issues of public concern. Here, one would conclude, *there is a role for the private business sector to play*.

Private companies face a number of limitations. Some stem from the competitive character and for-profit focus, others from the manner in which they elect to carry out their CCI roles.

- Almost all private companies that get involved in formal CCI activity confine this to communities where they have a business presence. There are a number of reasons for this. Part of what companies have to offer to the community is their employees, and employee morale is often one of the main reasons why a firm elects to engage in CCI programmes. Another reason is that companies feel they really know what might be best to do only where they have specific knowledge and experience, ie in communities where they have operations. A third factor is that companies need their licence to operate locally – political and social influence, connections, and a good image all help ensure this. This means that thousands of communities around the world – and in some instances major portions of whole countries – attract no interest because of the absence of a business presence of any particular note. This absence is most frequently evident in the poorest nations.
- Private businesses can be very particular about what they choose to support. They wish to enhance the reputation of their company, to promote brand identity. They want their logo attached to community projects they support. At times, they want to have exclusive ownership of a particular community issue or project in which they have a vested interest.
- By their very nature private businesses do not naturally choose to combine with other companies to address a community problem. The issue of education reform is a good example of this. A company arguing for reform is likely to do so from its particular vantage point: the question is 'what kinds of skill does my company need' not 'what kinds of skill do students in general need'. As a result, consensus as to what is important

proves illusive. Scarce financial and human resources are frittered away in small bites rather than on a scale that might lead to far greater impact. Ironically, businesses cooperate and combine all the time for the purpose of gaining strategic business advantage.

- Corporate attention to community issues can be rather fickle. Many companies do not wish to fund a particular issue for a long period of time. They can easily be dismayed at the lack of progress or conclude that no amount of support is likely to make any difference. A management change, changes in business ownership, or a decline in a business's fortunes can lead to substantial cuts in CCI budgets or a decision not to continue to fund issues that the company has historically supported.

- Companies tend to be risk-avoiding and likely to want to steer clear of supporting what they believe to be controversial social issues such as abortion, gay rights, human and civil rights, teenage pregnancy, abuse of women and children, diversity in the workplace, and family planning. This wariness can mean that important issues fall outside corporate attention even though many companies end up paying a high price for society's failure to resolve such issues.

- Companies are reticent about seeking and committing themselves to partnerships with NGOs. The 'we–they' character of project negotiations tends to introduce factors largely extraneous, and possibly inimical, to the resolution of social issues and the attainment of real progress.

These limitations, individually or collectively, do not diminish the need for the private company to play a role in building healthy communities. They are, however, real limitations, and need to be considered when reflecting on what the private company is likely to offer in the way of social improvement. I have tried to demonstrate throughout this work that when a company becomes more strategic in its CCI practices, relating these practices to its long-term business future and survival, it is more likely to expand its view of what it can bring to the community successfully, and in consequence be less risk-avoiding in its behaviour.

Is the growing influence of corporations corrupting the CCI process?

Corporations are gaining enormous economic power. At present the private sector accounts for over 93 per cent of capital flows to emerging economies. The largest 70 transnational corporations are bigger than most nation-states.

Countries and communities that depend on investment, whether from local or foreign sources, are subject to the inordinate influence that is exercised by companies, particularly large ones. Arriving with batteries of analysts, lawyers, engineers and high-powered executives, communities, even countries, are often overwhelmed. Frequently, these countries and communities do not have the skills and resources needed to negotiate effectively. I recall a case in Egypt in 1976 when the Egyptian government was presented with a 3,000-page sales contract from the Boeing Company for the purchase of aircraft. At that time, there were perhaps no more than five or six Egyptian lawyers who had any familiarity with American con-tract law. In the entire country, there were only six working telex machines, other than those in the military, available to the government and the public.

Communities often feel compelled to grant all sorts of concessions to firms they are seeking to attract. Tax holidays, personnel training at public expense, improvements in physical infrastructure, access to low-interest finance through industrial bonds, and the right to repatriate profits are but a few of the incentives commonly proffered. Corporations making invest-ments abroad, particularly in developing countries, often seek forms of market protection from potential competitors, either domestic or other for-eign companies. Companies have also been known to seek preferential treatment in relation to the taxes applied to imported parts and supplies needed for production. Finally, gaining the licence to operate in a country may involve payments to key individuals – politicians or government bureaucrats, the family members of prominent political or community lead-ers, and labour leaders.

Not every corporation takes advantage of all the offered incentives or indulges in corrupt practices such as pay-offs. Many companies have codes of conduct by which their shareholders, management and employees abide.

But corruption can be a way of doing business in many countries, including the industrialized nations, such as Japan. There are different cul-tural attitudes about what is an acceptable business practice. European companies feel that corporate bribes, especially in developing countries, are simply a cost of doing business. American businessmen often take the same position but are likely to be less open about it.

The main question is 'Do firms use their CCI actions to influence, bribe or corrupt?' Exercising corporate influence to obtain preferential conces-sions when negotiating with a non-profit partner must be distinguished from an effort to gain a similar business advantage by making payments to politicians or government officials. Nevertheless, a corporate contribution can be involved in either situation.

The use of influence in setting the terms of a corporate contribution

There are vast numbers of organizations seeking corporate support for countless causes and issues. In the USA, for example, there are over 1.5 million non-profit organizations addressing every conceivable cause and need. In Kenya, there are over 500 foreign NGOs registered that address all matter of issues.

Philanthropic organizations, whether private or corporate, can exercise a great deal of power. In South Africa, the Ford Foundation and IBM played significant roles, as did many other grant-making institutions and business corporations, in bringing about the economic boycott of the country and, ultimately, the political change that has taken place.

While, historically, corporations have tended to attach few conditions to their community investments or donations, there is a growing trend – an outgrowth of becoming 'strategic' – towards seeking certain conditions in return for corporate support. Firms like to receive acknowledgment, often by having their corporate name and logo displayed prominently at sponsored events or attached to a particular programme or gift, such as a minority scholarship or an endowed chair at a university.[14] But it can go further.

UNITED PARCEL SERVICE OF AMERICA (US)

United Parcel Service (UPS) is a mail, package and freight delivery company. In 1997 its revenues were $22.5 billion. It has 331,000 employees; it services the US domestic market and foreign markets worldwide.

In 1996 UPS-America offered the University of Washington School of Medicine a $2.5 million grant to establish an endowed research chair in occupational orthopaedics (*Wall Street Journal*, 6 February 1998). The gift was to be made through the UPS Foundation.

This is not an unusual practice in itself. Companies around the world endow university chairs. Foreign companies operating in major market areas often find this kind of action attractive. For example, Japanese corporations operating in the USA have been a major new source of endowed chairs over the past 15 years. In 1996 companies contributed almost $3 billion to higher education institutions.

While it is not unusual for the firm endowing an academic chair to specify the particular field in which the chair is to be established, such as foreign languages, medicine, economics or business, UPS wished to go further.

■ The company wanted a particular professor named to receive the chair and tenure. Such decisions are the receiving institution's prerogative, not that of the company making the donation, and this request triggered a strong reaction from university officials.

- The individual that UPS named, an orthopaedic specialist whose research 'suggested that workers' back-injury claims may relate more to poor attitudes than ergonomic factors on the job', made sense to the company. The company opposes government efforts to 'impose workplace ergonomics standards'. What better solution than to ask for a professor whose work supports an official company position?
- The paper trail on this transaction went straight to the point. In a memo from the company to the university we have: 'United Parcel Service asks for the opportunity to promote a specific programme at your institution by offering $2,500,000 in hopes of assuring our intentions – Advancing Dr Bigos' [the intended chair holder] research is *the only intention and motivation* [italics mine] for offering an endowment.'

This may seem a bit of a 'storm in a teacup'. However, there is a general concern in the USA that the growing dependence of universities on corporate largesse may be undermining their independence. This is a legitimate concern and, unfortunately for UPS, its attempt to exert influence ended up with the company being recognized, at least by the media, as a heavy-handed purveyor of money for education – as long as, and only if, its money served its own interests. UPS crossed the line. It did not attempt, however, to hide this fact. The gift was never made. The company and the university could not agree on the terms of the proposed chair. The UPS spin doctors tried to repair the damage. UPS terminated negotiations in 1997, noting that, 'for reasons having nothing to do with the merits', the offer was being withdrawn.

At best, UPS may simply have exercised bad judgement. Unfortunately for the company, it attempted to impose the terms of a gift at a time when the media was carrying any number of articles on the dangers of corporate financing of higher education.

The important message for corporations is that there are costs if they choose to over-specify the terms of what are supposed to be 'philanthropic' gifts. There *are* limits to serving self-interest.

There is a flip side to the issue of using CCI as a means of gaining benefits for the company providing the support. Community organizations and educational institutions can find their bargaining position strengthened in negotiating with businesses. In the USA this is certainly true for the prestigious universities such as Harvard, Stanford, Princeton or Duke. It can also be true for community service organizations. The United Way often receives preferential treatment from corporations that want communities around the USA to know that they are strong United Way supporters. Most Japanese companies engaging in CCI activities in the USA feel that it is imperative to support the United Way.

CCI as bribery

Some critics see CCI practices as just a form of bribery. The form this bribery takes may be subtle and seemingly well intended, but it is nevertheless bribery. Oil firms support environmental causes; tobacco firms charged with inducing teenage smoking support education; alcoholic beverage firms support driver training and Mothers Against Drunk Driving (MADD). To the critics, this is all evidence of hypocrisy at a minimum and at worst a way of buying off public criticism.

Bribery, at times involving the philanthropic arm of a company, can and does take place. In Japan until recently, when laws governing such payments changed, payments to individuals in political parties were considered a legal philanthropic expense and reported as such. In Egypt in the late 1970s and early 1980s, foreign corporations were pressed to make ostensibly philanthropic gifts to President Sadat's wife's favourite charity; it is suspected that funds contributed tended to end up in a Swiss bank account. Recently, Indonesia's former President Suharto was charged with plundering the assets of six charitable organizations run by members of his family. Any foreign corporation wishing to do business during his regime found it difficult to avoid supporting these charities, although there may have been some able to do so.

Companies use their philanthropic capacity to offset public resistance to their presence or environmental damage that may be caused by certain business practices. BP's explorations for oil in Colombia raised serious concerns, not only because these explorations would potentially alter the way of life for small isolated villages but also because it was not clear to the local population how it would benefit. BP initiated a microcredit project to build local communities' income-earning capacities and ultimately was able to bring in the World Bank to help link these locally based start-up enterprises to wider markets for their products.

A major US oil exploration and production corporation, Mobil Oil, experienced similar difficulties in Peru. The company is prospecting for oil deposits in the south-east Peruvian Amazon, where three 'uncontacted' (ie having little or no contact with the outside world) indigenous tribes reside. Charges have been made that through Mobil Oil employee contact with these tribes, diseases such as whooping cough and pneumonia have been introduced, with deadly results. In this instance, the company has not undertaken any CCI action to mitigate the situation, in part because 'contact' with the indigenous tribes is the issue. Also, the Mobil Foundation does not conduct operations outside the US.

Bribery occurs when an oil or any other company makes specific payments to circumvent particular laws that govern business practices. It is bribery when a company makes payments to officials for privileges or competitive advantage over others seeking to conduct business and play by established rules – rules ostensibly to be enforced by the government officials who accept these illegal payments.

Is this kind of bribery taking place, recognizing that in many countries it is ostensibly an 'accepted' method of doing business? Yes, it is, and it involves businesses that are considered quite reputable, and most probably are in many of their practices.

Do companies use their CCI activities for this kind of bribery? This is less clear. In cases where high-level political pressure is placed on companies to support a particular charity, which may be of dubious purpose and legitimacy, I am sure that the CCI arm may be engaged to make the donation or grant. I do not consider BP's effort to stimulate economic growth in rural communities in Colombia as bribery, even though it is designed to ease local resistance to the company's presence.

CCI actions as a penalty

Companies do redirect the programmes and objectives of their CCI practices to control the damage they may have done in the course of conducting business. A chemicals, pharmaceutical or oil company is acting in its self-interest by providing support for environmental education, health care and scientific research on an ongoing basis. The support provided may or may not mitigate the consequences of major industrial accidents or catastrophes. However, there is some evidence that when a company is visibly committed to issues of public concern, company managers and employees may exercise greater care in business operations.

When legal judgements are made against companies for unsafe business practices or environmental damage or public injury, it is not unusual for the courts to require contributions to be made to certain causes. This is a legal and not a company decision, although many companies against which such judgements have been made find themselves thinking more seriously about the CCI function and its usefulness in preventing and mitigating the consequences of future possible problems.

Examples of corporate contributions stemming from a business crisis – whether companies make them voluntarily or are required to do so by a legal judgement against them – are legion. The *Exxon Valdez* oil spill, Union Carbide's Bhopal incident, the spate of human injury incidents that grew out of adverse reactions to drugs and other medical procedures – thalidomide, breast implants, and the Dalcon Shield – Royal Dutch Shell's subsidiary Shell UK's *Brent Spar* problem, Ford Motor's Pinto gas bladder and the spacecraft *Challenger*'s O-rings all come to mind.

Integration of CCI in the corporation: changing corporate behaviour

An American Express executive, Harvey Golub, once said: 'Citizenship has two elements: the behaviour of a corporation as an entity and the behaviour of individuals in that entity.' A corporation, 'as an entity or through individuals in that entity', can have a darker side.

Golub is right in pointing out that while corporations may be legally designated anonymous entities, they are run by individuals. One outcome of a company's decision to be more strategic in its CCI practices is the need to involve all major departments, divisions, line and service functions, and ultimately shareholders, suppliers and customers, in the execution of its corporate responsibility. It is implicit in the term strategic.

A shareholders' revolt of sorts at the recent Annual Meeting of the Exxon Corporation, another giant US oil exploration and production company, typifies the difficulties involved in having a corporate policy that is inconsistent with the company's CCI effort. The Exxon Education Foundation and the Exxon Corporate Giving Programme both emphasize support for environmental education. At the April 1998 meeting, Exxon management attempted to keep the Interfaith Center on Corporate Responsibility (ICCR) from posing a resolution requiring the company to take stock of the impact of global warming on its policies and operations. Management did not succeed and more than 4 per cent of the shareholders voted against the company's position and in favour of the ICCR resolution.[15] Under Securities and Exchange Commission rules, this is enough to ensure that the ICCR-sponsored resolution must be entertained again at the next Annual Meeting.

Is the company that works assiduously to achieve company-wide integration of CCI more likely to avoid incidents and business practices that harm the company's reputation – harm that may prove costly in terms of legal judgements, lost customer confidence and erosion of employee morale and productivity? I conclude that it is.

One outcome of building a partnership between the Hitachi Foundation and the Hitachi corporation has been a significant reduction in the likelihood of ill-conceived business practices on the part of company employees. In the early 1980s, prior to formation of the Foundation, it was not unusual for the media to feature Hitachi Ltd as the very essence of the threat Japanese corporations posed to the dominance of the USA in world markets. The company had been involved in a number of dubious business practices, some of sufficient proportion to merit the criticism meted out by the media.

The Foundation was formed in 1985. By the late 1980s, media criticism of the Hitachi corporation had ceased. A number of positive articles, scrutinizing Hitachi's effort to be a 'good' corporate citizen, began to appear.

Before 1985 no Hitachi facility in the USA received any recognition for involvement in the community; indeed, few facilities were providing any support for community organizations. By the early 1990s 18 Hitachi facilities had received honours for community involvement, ranging from Corporation of the Year (Indiana) to United Way Campaign Company of the Year (in Santa Clara, California; Winston-Salem, North Carolina; and Harrodsburg, Kentucky).

A company's ability to organize its employees as representatives of the commitment to community is in that company's fundamental self-interest. It falls to the company to ensure its CCI practices are not so isolated from all other functions in the organization that the CCI is marginalized. In my opinion, making CCI a matter of business strategy does two things. It leads to ownership by the whole corporation of the benefits accruing from a sound approach to CCI. And, importantly, it leads to individual behaviour that projects and protects the citizenship reputation of the company. Organization-wide integration of the CCI function will not totally eliminate poor judgement or even outright illegal behaviour – emanating from either management or employees – but it can make it more easily detectable and therefore a less frequent occurrence.

6 The future of corporate citizenship, the future of capitalism

'Undeniably, corporations are the major force – political, social, environmental, cultural and economic – in the world today. Corporations are also the major obstacle to achieving some common vision of and action towards a sustainable society.'

Stephen Viederman, 'Multinational Corporations & Sustainable Development', *Values* (November 1997).

'All over the English-speaking world, and even tentatively in Germany, people are beginning to ask an elementary question. Who do companies belong to, and in whose interest should they be run?'

'Shareholder values', *The Economist* (10 February 1996).

'Something strange and wonderful is taking place in business – companies of all sizes and sectors are discovering that they function best when they merge their business interests with the interests of customers, employees, suppliers, neighbors, investors, and other groups, affected directly or indirectly by their operations.'

Joel Makower and Business for Social Responsibility, 'Taking Care of Business', in *Beyond the Bottom Line* (Touchstone, 1994).

There is not a single global problem – population, violence, racial tension, the environment, adequate housing, clean drinking water, inclusiveness amidst diversity and multiculturalism, the poorest of the poor, or access to a living – that would not benefit from the private sector's attention.

If private business is to contribute to resolving community issues and needs, how can we be sure that what it has to offer is effectively delivered? A strategic, self-interested business approach to CCI is likely to increase the effectiveness of a company's CCI activity as well as bringing benefits to the company bottom line.

If CCI programmes are run, so to speak, on the margins of the company's main activity, they will of necessity remain limited in effect. On the other hand, if they can affect the way companies do business and their corporate culture (relationships with shareholders, employees, customers, suppliers and communities), then companies can 'make a difference'. While the sums involved in CCI programmes are relatively small, companies' turnovers are huge. A strategic approach to CCI should enable the company to make a difference internally and externally, not just by aligning CCI actions with the company's business interest but by making CCI pervade the company's whole corporate culture, becoming part of the company's entire way of doing business.

In the USA many companies are attempting to make CCI strategic in the business sense. In Western European countries and Japan, there is somewhat less propensity for, or government support of, companies becoming involved in domestic social issues and public needs, so they don't get involved to any significant degree. Interestingly, within the European Union countries, companies from one country tend not to get involved in any of the others in which they have an established business presence. A German company does not engage in CCI through its operations in, say, France. A Dutch company does not feel compelled to be active in Italy.

Most emerging market economies do not make the support of community needs a condition of foreign investment approval. Many feel that they already have to bargain from a relatively weak position; politicians just want the jobs. Nevertheless, many companies making investments in these countries extend their practice of CCI. In such instances Western European companies are as likely as American companies to be strategic and self-interested in their support of emerging market communities.

Japanese companies remain more reticent in linking business purpose to CCI programmes carried out in developing countries than they are in the US. Private businesses originating in developing countries and engaged in community support activities are more likely to be doing this for purely communitarian and public interest purposes. However, if developing transnational corporations enter markets outside their home country, they too may find that linking business strategy with CCI is acceptable and worthwhile.

None of the logic of aligning CCI activity with business goals implies that being overly heavy-handed, bullying or cynical in its pursuit is acceptable. There are companies, and certain individuals within companies, who will always skate close to the edge. This is no less true in other kinds of organization.

A look to the future

There is a good deal of discussion about the future of capitalism. Recent events in Asia and Russia seemingly do not bode well, either for the continued expansion of capitalism or for continued public acceptance of capitalism's shortcomings. Can capitalism ever lead to the equitable distribution of wealth upon which its future will increasingly depend? Free-market operation on its own will do little to ensure this equity.

If one sees private CCI activity as at least one of the means by which equity can be improved, whether in the form of transfer of wealth or transfer of skills to enhance wealth, then I predict that a number of things will have to happen. I do not believe that businesses will abandon their quest to bring complementarity between the business's economic and social purposes, and to be strategic in doing this. If anything, I think we will see more companies, not just in the USA, attempting to do this. Private business takes its social mission far more seriously, and performs its CCI tasks better, when such a complementarity exists.

If further improvements in CCI performance are to be made, I think the following will have to happen:

- Substantial work will need to be done in educating shareholders on the need to move away from the present, very narrow definition of the purposes of business. Shareholders invest for a return, but they have to understand that this return is not necessarily going to be less because a firm chooses to advance improvements in community life. Study results show that the corporately responsible firm earns a higher return.

- Corporations worldwide have to take the need for volunteerism in communities far more seriously than they do at present. A good deal of lip-service is presently paid to this issue. Many firms advocate it only because they see it as a potential offset to cash expenditures for community improvement.

- Partnering – with other firms, NGOs, governments, other grant-making foundations – will have to move beyond the realm of rhetoric. The growing complexity of human and communal problems requires economies of scale, not the continued pursuit of a firm's ownership of only a small piece of a community problem.

- More constructive dialogue on the role of the private sector in improving social conditions is needed. At present, discussion centres far too much on criticizing business and very little energy is exerted attempting to engage business in the discussion.

- Firms must move away from expecting tax relief as the primary if not the sole motivation for supporting CCI programmes. If most of the major social ills that presently afflict nations are not resolved, these tax savings will pale in comparison to the costs of inaction that will visit companies' balance sheets.

- The needs of communities and nations that consistently fall outside the interests of the private sector must receive attention. To write them off solely because market size, disposable income and community or national asset base 'does not transact' in investment feasibility analysis is extremely short-sighted.

■ CCI programmes must squarely address the problem of the lack of employment opportunity and job security, particularly as it relates to dealing with the economic and social iniquities of the free-market system. When asked why he was paying $5 a day for unskilled help in the early 1900s – a time when such labour was paid $1 a day – Henry Ford replied, 'because people who make $5 a day buy cars'. Companies might want to bear this in mind.

Notes

1 David Logan, Delwin Roy and Laurie Regelbrugge (1997) *Global Corporate Citizenship: Rationale and strategies* The Hitachi Foundation.

2 *A Legal Guide for Investors in Guangdong and Hong Kong* (1995) Guangdong Provincial People's Protectorate and the Independent Commission Against Corruption, Hong Kong, pp 46-48.

3 Craig Smith in *Harvard Business Review*, May/June 1994.

4 For more information on this conference, see Laurie Vacek, *Corporate Citizenship in Asia Pacific: Summary report* (1997) Council on Foundations, Washington DC.

5 'Competitiveness and Corporate Social Responsibility', *Alliance*, March 1997; taken from Hampden-Turner and Tompenaars, *The Seven Cultures of Capitalism*.

6 *Measurement of Consumer Attraction to Socially Responsible Companies* (1994) Center for Corporate Community Relations, Boston College.

7 *RTZ: The Global Neighbour* (nd) RTZ Corporation plc, London.

8 *The Spirit of Giving: ARCO and the global community* (1997) ARCO, Los Angeles.

9 For a more detailed case study, see Logan et al, *Global Corporate Citizenship*, pp 145-149.

10 *The Road Ahead Programme: Microsoft in the community in Europe, Annual Report 1996/1997*, Microsoft Europe, Paris.

11 *BP in the Community: International report* (1997) The British Petroleum Company, London.

12 See Guillermo Jimenez, 'Case Study: Developing country projects funded by corporate Risk Fund', *Alliance*, April 1995.

13 Douglas P Woodward et al, *Foreign Direct Investment in Transitional Economies: The Coca Cola system in Poland and Rumania* (1995) International Business Program, College of Business Administration, University of South Carolina, Columbia, South Carolina, pp 7-10.

14 For example, see 'BMOC: Big money on campus. How private funding undercuts public education', *Washington Post*, 22 February 1998.

15 'Shareholders Defy Exxon over Global Warming Measure', *Washington Post*, 30 April 1998.

About CAF

CAF, the Charities Aid Foundation, is a registered charity with a unique mission: to do all in its power to ensure that the flow of resources to charities is as strong and effective as it can possibly be – worldwide. In all its activities CAF works to support a vibrant and effective non-profit sector.

In the UK, CAF provides a range of information, consultancy and money management services for individual and corporate donors and for charitable organizations. It handles over £600 million (US$1 billion) for more than 300,000 donors and several thousand charities. In 1996–97, it distributed over £150 million (US$240 million) to charities, including £5 million (US$8 million) to charities outside the UK.

CAF also has a major international role in providing information, advice and assistance to donors, charities and non-profit organizations (NPOs). CAF's international objectives are wide-ranging:

- to increase the scale of international philanthropy;
- to encourage the growth of philanthropy in different countries around the world;
- to build the capacity of NPOs;
- to build donor confidence in NPOs;
- to develop new forms of financing development activities and new systems of giving;
- to promote a more enabling legal and fiscal environment for the non-profit sector;
- to establish a core of knowledge about the workings of non-profit sectors around the world.

CAF is continually working to expand its international operation by developing new regional centres. CAF now has offices in Moscow, Washington DC, Brussels, Delhi and Johannesburg. Further expansion is being considered for a number of other countries. CAF's aim is to use the skills and experience developed in the UK to increase the flow of resources to the non-profit sector worldwide.

THE SERVICES CAF OFFERS

CAF offers a wide range of services for different client groups. These are available mainly in the UK, but for several years CAF has been exploring the possibilities of offering them in other countries.

Individual donors

Services to help individuals give more effectively include CAF's CharityCard, a debit card designed exclusively for tax-effective giving, the new World People card, and its Give As You Earn scheme, which enables people to make gifts direct from their pay. CAF can also help individuals establish trusts, make interest-free loans and leave legacies through their wills, and advise those who want to give across international boundaries.

Companies

Services for companies include CAF accounts for holding funds for corporate philanthropy, Give As You Earn and matched giving mechanisms. CAF now works with several major companies managing their corporate community involvement programmes on an international basis. CAF helps companies to give more effectively in countries in which they operate.

Major foundations

In the UK, CAF helped establish the community foundation movement, working in partnership with the American C S Mott Foundation. It was a founding member of the European Foundation Centre (EFC). CAF also has extensive experience of working with other foundations at project level.

Governments and international institutions

CAF has often worked with the UK government, but for several years this work has extended outside the UK. CAF has, for example, carried out work on behalf of the European Union; it is also working closely with the World Bank in Palestine.

Development of cross-border giving

In the UK, CAF has for many years worked to facilitate tax-effective donations overseas on behalf of its corporate and individual clients. CAFAmerica similarly encourages tax-effective gifts and grants from the USA and by US expatriates. In Europe, CAF played the lead role in establishing the Transnational Giving Agreement, to enable tax-effective donations to be made easily between parties in the UK, Belgium, Germany, France and the Netherlands.

Investment and money management for charities and non-profit organizations

In the UK, CAF offers four investment schemes tailored to charities' needs. The CafCash High Interest Cheque Account and the CAF Gold Account are instant access deposit accounts, while the CAF Income Fund and the CAF Balanced Growth Fund offer a choice of longer-term investment facilities.

Loan finance

For several years, CAF Loans Services has helped charities that need to borrow money. More recently, CAF has developed its own social investment fund, Investors in Society.

Administration and fundraising support

CAF can also help with charity administration, for example managing fundraising income and reclaiming tax where appropriate. It can administer major charitable appeals from start to finish.

Information and research services

CAF carries out extensive research in the UK and overseas. CAF Russia has published over 30 books, in English and Russian. In the UK, the focal point of the research programme *is Dimensions of the Voluntary Sector*, the definitive annual survey of the income and expenditure of the sector. Other initiatives supported by CAF include a major project to examine and develop the idea of benchmarking for charities and another to establish an accreditation system for charities.

Consultancy

CAF has been involved in many international projects on a consultancy basis, usually through CAF Consultants. This has, for example, involved working with the European Commission's Phare Civil Society Development Programme in Lithuania, Estonia and Latvia, and evaluating existing EC programmes in Bulgaria, Poland, the Czech Republic and Slovakia.

CAF Grants Council

Guided by an independent group of experts nominated by other voluntary organizations, the CAF Grants Council distributes around £400,000 (US$640,000) every year on behalf of CAF; it distributes much more on behalf of government, companies, foundations and other donors.

Charity Know How

Since 1991 CAF has administered the Charity Know How Fund, which contributes to the development of civil society in Central and Eastern Europe by supporting the revitalization of the non-profit sector in those countries. This programme has been recognized as a model of its type, with many hundreds of grants made to organizations in more than 20 different countries.

Working on the Internet

CharityNet is now one of the foremost guides to non-profit sector activity. In addition to an in-depth guide to all CAF activities, CharityNet includes CAF's international non-profit database of 70,000 organizations and CCINet, which brings together companies that have Internet space dedicated to their own corporate community activities.

For further information about CAF's international work, contact:
Andrew Kingman, International Development Director, CAF, Kings Hill, West Malling, Kent ME19 4TA, UK
Tel +44 1732 520119 *Fax* +44 1732 520100
E-mail akingman@caf.charitynet.org

Further information about all CAF's activities can be found on CharityNet, CAF's website, at: http://www.charitynet.org

Other publications from CAF

COUNTRY PROFILES

Introductory overviews of the non-profit sector in particular countries

Written in an easy journalistic style, these reports will help even the busiest executive to grasp quickly the key facts needed to make decisions on support for civil society and participatory development. Each explains the political and socio-economic environment, reviews the history and development of the non-profit sector, and evaluates its current situation – including the main areas of activity, funding sources, relations with national and local government, legal and fiscal environment, and the prime needs – before looking at the potential role of foreign donors and the challenges facing the various parts of the local sector.

The Non-Profit Sector in Bulgaria
ISBN 1-85934-059-8 £24.95 1998

The Non-Profit Sector in India
Michael Norton
ISBN 1-85934-023-7 £24.95 1996

The Non-Profit Sector in Russia
Paul LeGendre
ISBN 1-85934-036-9 £24.95 1997

The Non-Profit Sector in South Africa
Zane Dangor and the Development Resources Centre
ISBN 1-85934-024-5 £24.95 1997

SPECIAL REPORTS

HIV & AIDS in Russia
Darren Headley
ISBN 1-85934-015-6 £24.95 1996

Examines the official response to the appearance of HIV & AIDS and the role played by the emerging non-profit sector.

The Voluntary Sector in the European Union
Harry Kidd
ISBN 1-85934-030-X £24.95 1996

A country-by-country summary of the legal and fiscal framework applicable to associations, foundations and charities in all the member states.

Gays & Lesbians in Russia
Paul LeGendre
ISBN 1-85934-070-9 £24.95 1998

The first overview, with full statistical information, of the emerging homosexual community in post-communist Russia.

Building Civil Society: Current initiatives in voluntary action
Edited by Barry Knight, Matthew Smerdon and Cathy Pharoah
ISBN 1-85934-085-7 £9.99 1998

A collection of ten articles spotlighting new thinking about how communities can use their power and resources to address the problems which top-down initiatives often fail to solve.

JUST PUBLISHED

Companies in Communities: Valuing the contribution
David Logan and Michael Tuffrey
ISBN 1-85934-103-9 £29.95 1999

Until recently few companies were able to put an accurate figure on their community contribution – cash and non-cash – still less to say what it actually achieves for the company and the community. This practical guide, providing step-by-step guidance for community affairs managers undertaking a benchmarking exercise for the first time, will help solve this problem.

To order any of the above publications, please ring Biblios Publishers' Distribution Services Ltd on +44 1403 710 851

Index

American Express Company, US 16, 39–40, 41, 65
Apple Computer, US 16
Aracruz Cellulose SA, Brazil 13, 36–37, 56
ARCO *see* Atlantic Richfield Company
arts, funding 12, 13, 16
Atlantic Richfield Company (ARCO) 35–36
Ayala, Jaime Augusto Zobel de 24–25
Ayala Corporation, Philippines 13, 24

Bosch (Robert) GmbH 13
BP *see* British Petroleum 63
bribery 11, 60, 63–64
British Petroleum (BP), UK 32, 44–45, 52, 63, 64
business strategies 7–8, 17, 33, 65, 66, 67–68

California Community Foundation 8
Caltex Companies 32
Canon 32
capital/capital goods transfers 12
Cathay Pacific 32
cause-related marketing 8, 10, 16, 26, 27, 41–46
Chan, Ronnie 7, 24
chemicals firms 34, 43–44, 45–46, 64
China 11, 38, 46, 49, 56
Ciba-Geigy Corporation, Switzerland 13, 18, 41, 45–46
clothing companies 13, 18, 42–43, 54–56
Coca Cola Company, US 18, 32, 46–47
codes of conduct 60
conditions, setting 61–62

consumer loyalty 37–38
contacts, establishing 9
cooperation, need for 58–59
   see also partnerships, building
corporate community involvement (CCI):
   limitations 58–59
   methods used 11–13
   reasons for 7, 9–10, 25–26
corruption 60, 66
   see also bribery
cultural differences 9, 10–11, 26

developing countries 46, 59–60, 68
direct marketing 9, 25
disease, campaigns against 41, 45–46
donations 12, 16
drug companies *see* pharmaceutical companies

Eastern Europe 32, 46–47
educational issues 8, 10, 13, 18, 32, 58, 61–62
Egypt 45, 46, 49, 60, 63
ELF-Aquitaine 13
employees, company 58, 65, 66, 67
   matching funds programmes 11
   payroll giving 12
   volunteers 9, 10, 12, 13, 42, 69
environmental issues 14, 17, 32, 34, 38, 41–42, 63, 64
   and extractive industries 33–37, 63
European Union 68
expertise, provision of 12
Exxon Corporation 14, 17, 38, 64, 65

Ford Foundation 61
foreign markets 8–9, 30
   gaining acceptance in 49–53
   see also Japanese corporations, US-based

France 10, 18, 32
free-market operations, developing 46–48
Fuji Xerox Co, Japan 25

General Electric 14
globalization 16–17, 24
Golub, Harvey 65
Grand Metropolitan plc, UK 52–53
grants 11
Guatemala: PVH plants 55

Haas, Robert 56
Hall, Mary Stewart 7
Handy, Charles 7
Hang Lung Development Group, Hong Kong 7, 24
health care 10, 11, 41, 44–46, 64
Hewlett-Packard, US 13, 16
Hitachi Group of Companies 18, 27, 52
   Hitachi America Ltd (HAL) 50
   Hitachi Corporation 32
   Hitachi Foundation 7, 18, 27, 31, 43, 50, 51–52, 65–66
   Hitachi Ltd, Japan 13, 27, 50, 65
Honda Motor Corporation 13
Hongkong and Shanghai Bank 32
human rights issues 54, 55, 56

IBM 16, 18, 32, 61
ICWI Group, Jamaica 13
India 46, 49
Indonesia 35–36, 45, 46, 63
Interfaith Center on Corporate Responsibility 65
Ireland 38–39

Japan External Trade Organization (JETRO) 13
Japanese corporations 10–11, 13, 16, 60, 63, 68
   irresponsible 14
   US-based 11, 13, 27–28, 30, 31, 61, 62, *see also* Hitachi Foundation

Kenya 45, 61
Klatsky, Bruce 54-56
Kobayashi, Yotaro 25
Koc Group, Turkey 13

Levi-Strauss & Company 13, 18, 56
licences to operate, acquiring 18, 33–37, 58, 60
loan funds, community development 48

Makower, Joel 67
market protection 60
Marks & Spencer 13
Marsden, Chris 9, 10, 26, 57
medical research, funding 13
   see also pharmaceutical companies
mentoring services 12
Merck & Company, US 13, 41
Mexico 43–44, 46, 49
microcredit projects 12, 63
Microsoft Corporation, US 38–39
mining corporations 33–35
Mobil Oil, US 63
Monsanto Company, US 43–44, 56
Morita, Akio 28

NEC, Japan 31
Nestlé (Thailand) Ltd, Switzerland 47–48
NGOs/NPOs 61
   partnering 10, 59, 69
   supporting 10, 11, 12

office space and supplies, provision of 12
oil companies 14, 33, 35–36, 38, 63, 64, 65

Pagerungan Island, Indonesia 35–36
Panasonic Foundation 27, 31
partnerships, building 10, 59, 69
pay-offs 60
payroll giving systems 12
pharmaceutical companies 13, 34,

41, 43, 45–46, 64
Philippines 13, 14, 24
Phillips-Van Heusen Corporation, US
     54–56
Pillsbury Foundation, US 52, 53
Poland 32
political pressures 63, 64
printing and publication services 12
PVH *see* Phillips-Van Heusen

Regelbrugge, Roger 14
reputations, corporate 9, 54, 58
research and development 32, 34, 41
resource bases, protecting 33–37
Rio Tinto plc, UK 34–35
Rockefeller Foundation 43, 44
Romania 32, 47
Royal Dutch Shell Oil 14, 38, 64

scholarships, provision of 13, 61
school-to-work programmes 12, 32
Shakely, Jack 8
shareholders 7, 65, 67, 69
social issues 10, 18, 32, 41–42, 57,
     69
   controversial and unpopular 31,
        59, 69
   and limitations of corporate
        responsibility 58–59
   see also health care; unemployment
Sony Corporation, Japan 27–28
South Africa 44–45, 61
sponsorships 12, 16, 61
sports sponsorship 12, 16
strategies *see* business strategies
student exchange programmes 13
Suharto, President 63
Sung-Joo Han 24
supplies, provision of 12

tax incentives 11, 15–16, 60, 69
teacher exchange programmes 13
technical assistance, provision of 12
Texaco, US 38
Thailand 48
timber industry 33, 36–37
Timberland Company, US 42–43
Toshiba, Japan 31
tourist industry 39–40
transgenics 43–44
transportation services 12

unemployment 32, 38–39, 70
Union Carbide: Bhopal incident 14,
     64
United Parcel Service of America
     61–62
United States 10, 11, 18, 26, 28–30,
     60, 61, 68
   consumer loyalty 37–38
   Foreign Corrupt Practices Act 11
   Japanese firms 11, 13, 27–28, 30,
        31, 49, 61, 62, *see also* Hitachi
        Foundation
   taxation 15, 16
   UK firms 49, 52–53
United Way 62
university chairs 61–62

Viederman, Stephen 67
volunteers, employee 9, 10, 12, 13,
     69

Wal-Mart Stores Inc, US 19
Whirlpool Corporation, US 20–23
World Business Council for
     Sustainable Development 32

Yankelovich Monitor 28, 29